A READER'S GUIDE TO
TRANSFORMING MISSION

The American Society of Missiology Series, published in collaboration with Orbis Books, seeks to publish scholarly works of high merit and wide interest on numerous aspects of missiology — the study of Christian mission in its historical, social, and theological dimensions. Able presentations on new and creative approaches to the practice and understanding of mission will receive close attention from the ASM Series Committee.

American Society of Missiology Series, No. 37

A READER'S GUIDE TO
TRANSFORMING MISSION

Stan Nussbaum

Maryknoll, New York 10545

Founded in 1970, Orbis Books endeavors to publish works that enlighten the mind, nourish the spirit, and challenge the conscience. The publishing arm of the Maryknoll Fathers and Brothers, Orbis seeks to explore the global dimensions of the Christian faith and mission, to invite dialogue with diverse cultures and religious traditions, and to serve the cause of reconciliation and peace. The books published reflect the views of their authors and do not represent the official position of the Maryknoll Society. To learn more about Maryknoll and Orbis Books, please visit our website at www.maryknoll.com.

To learn more about Global Mapping International, the organization for which Stan Nussbaum is staff missiologist, visit their website, www.gmi.org.

Library of Congress Cataloging-in-Publication Data

Nussbaum, Stan.
    A reader's guide to Transforming mission / Stan Nussbaum.
      p. cm. – (The American Society of Missiology series)
    Includes index.
    ISBN 1-57075-594-9 (pbk.)
    1. Bosch, David Jacobus. Transforming mission. 2. Missions – Theory.
3. Missions – Theory – History of doctrines. 4. Christianity and other
religions. I. Title. II. Series.
BV2063.N87 2005
266'.001 – dc22

                    2004024002

This book is dedicated to
Leaderwell Pohsngap
and all those around the world like him
who long for mission to become central
to theological education in a new era

Contents

PART ONE
NEW TESTAMENT PARADIGMS

PART TWO
PARADIGMS IN CHURCH HISTORY

Lists of Figures and Tables

LIST OF FIGURES

LIST OF TABLES

Preface to the ASM Series

The purpose of the ASM (American Society of Missiology) series is to publish — without regard for disciplinary, national, or denominational boundaries — scholarly works of high quality and wide interest on missiological themes from the entire spectrum of scholarly pursuits relevant to Christian mission, which is always the focus of books in the series.

By *mission* is meant the effort to effect passage over the boundary between faith in Jesus Christ and its absence. In this understanding of mission, the basic functions of Christian proclamation, dialogue, witness, service, worship, liberation, and nurture are of special concern. And in that context questions arise, including, How does the transition from one cultural context to another influence the shape and interaction between these dynamic functions, especially in regard to the cultural and religious plurality that comprise the global context of Christian mission?

The promotion of scholarly dialogue among missiologists and among missiologists and scholars in other fields of inquiry may involve the publication of views that some missiologists cannot accept and with which members of the Editorial Committee do not agree. Manuscripts published in the series reflect the opinions of their authors and are not understood to represent the position of the American Society of Missiology or of the Editorial Committee. Selection is guided by such criteria as intrinsic worth, readability, and accessibility to a range of interested persons and not merely to experts or specialists.

The ASM Series, in collaboration with Orbis Books, seeks to publish scholarly works of high merit and wide interest on numerous aspects of missiology — the scholarly study of mission. Able presentations on new and creative approaches to the practice and understanding of mission will receive close attention.

The ASM Series Committee
JONATHAN J. BONK
ANGELYN DRIES, O.S.F.
SCOTT W. SUNQUIST

xiii

Preface

One of the greatest privileges of my life was to study under David Bosch at the University of South Africa while I was working with African indigenous churches in neighboring Lesotho. Whenever I pick up *Transforming Mission,* I hear him talking, just as we talked at his home and in his office. That book has become the most widely used mission textbook in the world, but many readers who never had the privilege of his personal teaching do not find his book as clear and easy to follow as I do. This book is designed to make it easier for them to hear Bosch, benefit from him, and challenge him.

Brevity, clarity, and accuracy have been my goals. While reducing the text by about 80 percent, I have simplified the vocabulary, used shorter sentences and paragraphs, added diagrams, tables, analogies, and discussion questions, and reorganized some of the chapters internally. I have tried to present Bosch's main ideas and the flow of his thought, confining my own opinions to occasional footnotes and a longer section in chapter 14.

If *Transforming Mission* is a tour through a game park, this book is a quick, low-altitude plane flight over the park. It reveals some of the same things as a trip on the park trails, but they all pass by very quickly. Though a few tourists may be content with the plane ride, its main value for most people will be helping them find the parts of the park where they want to spend more time exploring the terrain as mapped by Bosch himself in *Transforming Mission.*

To help the reader move easily from this book to Bosch a precise method of page referencing, using tenths of a page, has been employed. For example, the reference "(103.1)" in this book means the desired text is in the first tenth of page 103 of Bosch, that is, roughly the first five lines. "103.9" means the reference is to the last five lines on that page, "103.5" means it is in the middle of the page, etc.

In writing a book to introduce *Transforming Mission,* I have felt like I suppose a woman feels when trying to apply nail polish with a three-inch-wide brush. No matter how careful she is, something is bound to get smeared. I am sure I have smeared some things here. Perhaps with the help of my readers, I may correct some of them in a future edition. Thank you for your comments and your forgiveness in the meantime. As the Basotho say, *Thupa e otlolloe e sa le metsi* (The walking stick may be straightened while it is still green). You can contact me with corrections and suggestions at the following e-mail address: swnussbaum@gmi.org.

STAN NUSSBAUM

Acknowledgments

Of the many who deserve to be thanked for their assistance and encouragement on this project, let me begin with eight friends at *Union Biblical Seminary* in Pune, India, who represent the group I hope will benefit most from the book — mission students and mission teachers in the Two-Thirds World. *Dr. Leaderwell Pohsngap,* UBS principal, graciously agreed to let me test my draft there with the help of faculty members *Ebenezer Dasan* and *Hetoni Swu* (both working on Ph.D.s) and five master's degree students — *Nengkhovei Haokip, Akho Angami, John Philip, Jonathan Chang,* and *Meyingangla Ao.* During a four-day seminar in November 2003 these friends read the draft, made notes for me, and attended my lecture and discussion sessions. Their feedback was extremely helpful.

Other field tests of the draft were carried out by:

- *Hwa Yung,* director of the Centre for the Study of Christianity in Asia, Trinity Theological College, Singapore, "Theology of Mission" course for master's students.

- *Cathy Ross* (Bible College of New Zealand), visiting lecturer at Uganda Christian University, third year B.D. class in "Christian Mission" and first year MA (theology) class, "Theory and Practice of Mission in the 21st Century."

- *Bonnie Sue Lewis,* Associate Professor of Mission and Native American Christianity, University of Dubuque Theological Seminary, seminar on "Today's Missionaries" and class, "History of Christian Mission."

Very helpful comments were received from two other lecturers who have regularly used Bosch, though a field test of my draft did not fit into their teaching schedule in autumn 2003: *Frances Oborji* (Rome) and *William Daniel* (Atlanta).

As I hope the work will also be useful to mission executives and administrators, I invited several to review the draft. Thanks to *Charles Bennett,* Partners International (retired), *Art Brown,* Free Methodist World Mission, *Gary Hipp,* Moving Mountains, and *John Morehead,* Watchman Fellowship, for their perspectives and encouragement.

Last but not least among the readers is *Anjila Sisler,* an American veterinarian with no formal training in theology or mission. However, she has an exceptionally good eye for spotting the places where her father's manuscripts need clarification for the ordinary reader. Thanks, Anji.

Annemie Bosch, a friend for more than two decades, gave her blessing to the project early on. *Bill Burrows,* editor of Orbis Books, has given his wholehearted support as well. *Global Mapping International* allocated many of my working days for the writing; thanks to all the individuals and congregations whose donations to GMI made this possible. *Ferne Weimer,* director of the *Billy Graham Center Library* in Wheaton, provided major help with information for some of the biographical sketches in Appendix B, as did Christof Sauer at the University of South Africa. I also used the library at *Trinity Theological College,* Singapore. *Sam O'Rear* effectively translated my rough sketches into the sharp and clear diagrams included in this book.

To all these friends and to God their Father I give my hearty thanks. May this book, in spite of its remaining weaknesses, serve its purpose in the *missio Dei.*

A READER'S GUIDE TO
TRANSFORMING MISSION

Introducing David Bosch, His Context, Assumptions, and Agenda

His context

As a Dutch Reformed Afrikaaner whose ministry career spanned roughly the apartheid era of South African history (1948–94), David Bosch lived, thought, and wrote in a crucible. Permanently out of step with his church and his government, he was watched closely and attacked by both but never successfully manipulated or controlled by either. In this he embodied the style of discipleship Jesus advocated: sent out as a sheep among the wolves, he was as shrewd as a snake and as innocent as a dove (Matt. 10:16). He did not seek to overthrow unjust authorities but to undermine them by pursuing his real mission in spite of them. Therefore, in the completely polarized society of South Africa at the time, the radicals accused him of being too mild and the conservatives of being too radical.

Several times he considered leaving his church, and at least once he considered leaving his country (for an attractive teaching post overseas). But he always decided that God wanted him to remain an insider, an uncompromising Christian in a highly compromised situation. He lived what he advocated so often in his writing — "creative tension" between apparently irreconcilable opposites.

For the last two decades of his life, his working context was the missiology department in the faculty of theology of the University of South Africa (Unisa) in Pretoria. This was a unique situation in several respects. Though apartheid laws prohibited black and white students from sharing a university dormitory or cafeteria, Unisa was multiracial because it had no resident students. It was a correspondence school established a century earlier to make training available to those who were out of reach of any campus, and it had developed probably the highest academic standards of any correspondence institution in the world, from bachelor's through doctoral level.

The university was phenomenally well funded and subsidized in the apartheid era. For example, with moderate grant assistance, Bosch was able to edit and produce the premier journal *Missionalia,* providing the world's best set of abstracts of mission-related articles. Tuition fees at the university were unbelievably low (about $200 per year in 1979, when I began my doctoral program there), and that included Bosch as personal supervisor, two other faculty supervisors, and an amazing array of library services by mail. Black students could afford to study there, and they did.

Partly for this reason, theologians with anti-apartheid leanings tended to gravitate to this institution where they would not experience the hostility that was common in the theology departments at white campuses and church-controlled seminaries. Naturally the government was unhappy about this growing nest of vipers, yet it did not want to cut the funding for the university since the massive faculty building and library atop a ridge in Pretoria were an exhibit of how well the government provided educational opportunities for "our black people." The government resorted to other means, going as far as trying to assassinate Bosch's right-hand man, Willem Saayman, in his bed, but the rifle bullet hit the headboard on his wife's side of the bed, and she had not come to bed yet.[1]

In such an atmosphere, the common attempts by conservative South African Christians to separate religion from politics could not be reconciled with the Bible as Bosch read it. His own hermeneutic always was grounded in the way the biblical writers saw themselves, and that excluded any interpretation or application of particular Bible verses that went against the core identity and mission of the writers. For example, no one should suggest that the church turn a blind eye to injustice as if that were none of its business.

One side effect of his time and place was that because of his South African passport, Bosch though a world traveler had virtually no experience of Africa outside of southern Africa. He did manage to get a special visa to participate in the Pan African Christian Leadership Assembly in Nairobi in 1976, but that was a rare exception. He was quite involved in global meetings, both ecumenical and evangelical, and was fluent in English, Dutch, German, Afrikaans, and Xhosa, a major South African language he used during his years of teaching at a seminary for black ministers in the Transkei region.

Bosch considered South Africa an excellent vantage point from which to address both Europe and North America, drawing on both but keeping enough distance to think independently. Another advantage of a South African perspective was that mission was not an "overseas" matter. It was easier for the South African church than for the European and American churches to recognize the congruence between the local, regional, and global aspects of mission. A third advantage was that the racial mix in South Africa (about 15 percent white and 85 percent other) was similar to the ratio of Westerners to non-Westerners globally. The racial inequality issues that South Africa has been dealing with are likely to become worldwide issues as globalization increases and the non-Western poor assert themselves against their current abuse by the rich in the West.

---

1. The shooter confessed years later to the Truth and Reconciliation Commission.

His assumptions

Transforming Mission must be read in light of Bosch's basic assumptions, some of which are not explicitly stated in his book:

1. We are at a major transition point in world history, which means that Christian mission must also undergo a major transition in form, though it will never be swallowed up in pluralism (introduction and chap. 11).

2. The "crisis" in mission is essentially a crisis in the Western countries that have been the bases for Christian mission in the past four centuries (introduction).

3. The "mission" we seek to (re)model and carry on is the mission that started with Jesus' announcement of the arriving reign of God; the Old Testament is built on a different model of relationship with God that is not so intrinsically missionary in nature (chap. 1).[2]

4. Paradigm theory provides the best framework for studying transitions in mission from one era to the next (chap. 5). The Enlightenment, the paradigm that has dominated our age, is losing its grip on the world, but is still the paradigm we most need to recognize, understand, and move beyond as we shape our new view of mission (chaps. 9–10).

5. Our best chance of recognizing the Enlightenment's influence on our mission thought and practice is to get a broad biblical and historical perspective on mission by looking at several other models or paradigms (chaps. 1–9).

6. The new paradigm is not a complete rejection of the old; there will be some continuity as well as some major changes (chap. 11).

7. The three main theological streams we most need to take into account as we struggle toward a new paradigm of mission are Roman Catholic, ecumenical Protestant, and evangelical Protestant; Orthodox and charismatic streams do not figure prominently (chap. 12).

8. The biggest single challenge in forming a new paradigm for mission is to take ideas long considered to be incompatible opposites and hold them together in "creative tension" (chap. 12).

9. The best we can do at this point in history is identify a number of the pieces we are fairly sure will have a place in the puzzle of our new paradigm of mission; we cannot fit them all neatly together, and we may not even have all the pieces yet (chaps. 12–13).

---

2. Bosch's view was that Israel's mission was centripetal, that is, attracting other nations to God by modeling life as a society under God's rule. The church's mission is centrifugal, commanding Christians to go out among the nations and spread God's good news and grace everywhere.

His agenda

Bosch's deepest concern is with the way Western Protestants have seen themselves and their mission. He believes that in the modern era they have become unnecessarily polarized into evangelical and ecumenical camps and psychologically distanced from the Two-Thirds World because of the influence of the Enlightenment. Each camp has a part of the truth but has developed its theology and programs in a lopsided manner. If they can now reintegrate their complementary parts of the truth around the original kingdom-centered message of Jesus and the New Testament writers, they can reformulate their mission in an appropriate way for the new postmodern era of history.

When Western Christians do this, they will discover that they are not the saviors of the world but participants with Christians of all nations in the mission of God. It is certainly bigger than the Western church and even in some sense bigger than the whole global church. Bosch wants to stretch them toward a view of mission that is not Western-centered.

He thus provides a view of mission that is of immense interest to the global church today, especially the less Westernized parts of it. His suggestions feed into the global formulation of a missiology not dominated by the Enlightenment paradigm. He has not finished the job, and he knows it, but that was not his intention. He wanted to help create the biblical and historical foundations and bring some of the building materials to the site. The actual construction of the new paradigm will require a whole work crew.

His death

In April 1992, two years before the end of apartheid, Bosch tragically bled to death after a head-on traffic accident in a rural area of South Africa. Passersby called for an ambulance to bring the "jaws of life" and cut his feet free so the bleeding could be stopped. When they called a second time to ask what was taking so long, the emergency dispatcher reportedly replied, "You didn't say he was a white man." A later investigation of whether this actually occurred was inconclusive, largely because the tapes of the two phone conversations had disappeared.

How ironic that one who lived as an enemy of racism should die as an unofficial victim of it. But racism was not the victor in this story. Bosch's death exposed racism for what it really is — an ideology that kills even when it does not intend to, an ideology that cannot silence those it wishes to silence. How could it, when mere death is its ultimate weapon?

YOUR VIEWS AND YOUR CONTEXT

1. Suppose you attended a lecture in which Bosch stated his assumptions as they are listed above. Choose one assumption you would you want to hear him clarify or defend. What would you ask him about it?

Bosch's Introduction to Transforming Mission

Is Christian Mission a Thing of the Past?

(Bosch, TM, pp. 1–11)

"The Christian mission is in the firing line today," and the attack on it is coming from inside the church as well as outside (2.3).[1] Consider the ways the world has changed since the mid-twentieth century when mission still was accepted as a normal part of life by the church and the wider world (3.3):

- Science and technology have made huge advances, which many have interpreted to mean that humans can manage everything very well without God.

- The "Christian" West has seen massive declines in church membership.

- People of other faiths have moved into "Christian" countries in large numbers.

- Western Christians have come to feel increasingly guilty as they realize how un-Christian their nations were in the colonial period.

- The gap between rich and poor has widened, leaving the rich Christians uncertain whether they have any credibility with the angry poor.

- Western theology is being challenged by a number of theologies based in the experience of other parts of the world.

This combination of things has exposed some serious weaknesses in widely held beliefs about the foundation, aim, and nature of mission (4.8). Chief among these was the assumption that Western culture, because it was superior to all others, would be the bucket that would carry the life-giving water of the gospel all over the world. Other religions would fade away as people realized the superiority

---

1. Page number format: a number such as "2.3" means that the quotation is from page 2 of Bosch and can be found 3/10 of the way down the page. There are approximately five lines per tenth of a page.

Table 1
A Graphic Outline of *Transforming Mission*

Biblical	Historical	Today
Part 1, Ch. 1-4, pp. 15-178	Part 2, Ch. 5-9, pp. 181-345	Part 3, Ch. 10-13, pp. 349-519

		10. Enlightenment unraveling
	5. Paradigm theory	11. Church and mission in flux
	6. **Eastern Orthodox** Patristic period, 100-600, Jn. 3:16	
1. **New Testament** model(s)	7. **Roman Catholic** Middle Ages, 600-1500, Lk. 14:23	12. **An emerging paradigm**
	8. **Protestant** (part 1) Reformation, 1500-1800, Ro. 1:16-17	
2. Matthew 3. Luke 4. Paul	9. **Protestant** (part 2) Enlightenment & modern era, 1800-2000, Mt. 28:18-20, Lk. 4:18-19	13. Mission in many modes

Notes

1. The six main paradigms of mission are shown in bold type

2. Size of boxes shows relative size of Bosch's chapters and sections

of Christianity, and we would end up with a Christian world by the end of the twentieth century (6.5).

The global changes and the exposed mistakes in mission aims and practice have led to two opposite reactions among Christians. One is "a terrible failure of nerve about the missionary enterprise," leading to "an almost complete paralysis and total withdrawal" from anything that smacks of mission at all (6.9). The other is to ignore the new trends, deny the crisis, and carry on using the old colonialist model of mission as if nothing has changed (7.2).

"The thesis of this book [is] that the events we have been experiencing at least since World War II and the consequent crisis in Christian mission are not to be understood as merely incidental and reversible. Rather, what has unfolded in theological and missionary circles during the last decades is the result of a fundamental paradigm shift, not only in mission or theology, but in the experience and thinking of the whole world" (4.4).

If that thesis is correct, we should neither withdraw from mission nor keep using the old methods. "Rather, we require a new vision to break out of the present stalemate toward a different kind of missionary involvement" (7.8). "The harsh realities of today compel us to re-conceive and reformulate the church's mission, to do this boldly and imaginatively, yet also in continuity with the best of what mission has been in the past decades and centuries" (8.3).

To achieve this we need to consider both the variety of the models of mission in the New Testament itself and other models that have emerged as the church has faced four previous experiences of paradigm shift in the world around it. As shown in Table 1, the New Testament and church history will each take about one-third of the book. In the final third, we will look at the current situation and the way to make the paradigm shift of our own era.

Before launching our investigation, we must state some assumptions and convictions that will be explained in greater detail as we go along (8.7):

- The Christian faith is "intrinsically missionary" (8.9). Christian mission starts with God on a mission, especially in Jesus Christ (9.5). If Christian mission is a thing of the past, so is the Christian faith, for it is faith in the reign of God through Jesus Christ over all humanity and all creation (9.8).

- Missiology studies mission not in theoretical objectivity but from the perspective of commitment to the Christian, missionary faith. This commitment does not blind us to the faults of mission but intensifies our desire to find and correct those faults (9.3).

- We will never arrive at a perfect definition of mission (9.4). The Bible will give us guidance but no magic formulas for mission (9.7). The church in its mission is a sign of the kingdom but never a perfect embodiment of it (11.6).

- If a church defines mission only in terms of this-worldly activities like promoting justice or only in terms of saving souls for the world to come, it is not being true to the true God. His mission has both worlds clearly in view (10.6, 10.7, 10.9, 11.1).

• The difference between home and foreign missions is artificial (9.9). The difference between mission and "missions" is crucial. "Mission" refers to God's own mission in which the church participates and to which it points. "Missions" refers to particular forms of mission the church develops in specific circumstances (10.4).

YOUR VIEWS AND YOUR CONTEXT

2. Bosch drafted this material in about 1990. Which if any of his assumptions (above or in the list on p. 5) need to be revised in light of what has happened since then? How should they be revised?

3. Bosch wrote as a South African with a global audience in mind. How well do his assumptions fit your particular country or region? How might you edit them in order to provide a better starting point for a theology of mission where you are?

PART ONE

NEW TESTAMENT
PARADIGMS

Chapter 1

The New Testament
as a Missionary Document

(Bosch, TM, pp. 15–55)

The original audience for the New Testament writings was not a catechism class or a seminary. It was an entire religious movement living a missionary life, spreading a missionary message, and along the way running into one crisis after another. The early church, "because of its missionary encounter with the world, was *forced* to theologize" (16.4). It had to find some answers to the burning questions raised by announcing the gospel in non-Christian, even non-Jewish, settings. To look into the New Testament for guidance about mission today is therefore completely in keeping with the nature of the writings themselves.

The Old Testament writings were not as pervaded with this missionary nature, but they did provide some essential starting points for New Testament mission. First, the God of the Old Testament is a God who steps into the flow of human history in ways of his choosing, unlike the gods of other nations who were tied to the annual seasonal cycle and to certain religious centers and rites (17.4). Second, revelation from this God is frequently a revelation of what he is promising to do for people at a later stage of history, not simply what religious acts he expects people to do for him today (17.9). Third, God focuses his involvement in history and his promises on one nation, Israel, which he brought into being and appointed for a special type of service as his representative among the nations (18.3).

New Testament mission combines all three of these ideas. The sending of Jesus is presented as another example of God stepping into history and changing its course. It was also the fulfillment of the many promises of the coming Messiah, and it was the ultimate example of something happening in Israel that had global implications.

How do we bridge from mission then to mission now? Many scholars have dismissed the historical value of the New Testament writings and gone on to invent all kinds of Jesus figures as props for their predetermined views of mission (22.1). Others have got hung up on an "objective reality" that supposedly is not affected by the interpretation of the observer (24.4). Many mission promoters have tried to apply the words of the New Testament writings straight to mission today without taking the original context into account.

A sounder approach is that of "critical hermeneutics" (23.8), which asks how the writers understood themselves and their situations and how this affected their interpretations of Jesus. "They handled the traditions about [Jesus] with creative but responsible freedom, retaining those traditions while at the same time adapting them" (21.6). "A crucial task for the church today is to test continually whether its understanding of Christ corresponds with that of the first witnesses" (22.7). This is the other half of critical hermeneutics, how we understand ourselves.

In the next three chapters we will consider the self-understanding of Matthew, Luke, and Paul and its impact on their writings. Before going into those details we need to look at the self-understanding of Jesus, insofar as we can fathom it from his circumstances and the writings about him.

JESUS' OWN PERSON AND MINISTRY

Jesus clearly did not see himself as a religious teacher with a generic message of religious truth for all humanity (20.5). "He stands in the tradition of the [Old Testament] prophets. Like them and John the Baptist his concern is the repentance and salvation of Israel" (26.4).

In one important sense, however, his strategy for prophetic ministry went against the grain of all other Jewish movements of his day. For all the others, the prophetic task was to define the faithful remnant and build walls around it to keep it from being polluted and lost. The Pharisees and especially the Essenes set about this with great dedication. Even the baptism of John was a way of defining a boundary between ordinary Jews and the true Jews who would be saved by the Messiah (25.7).

Jesus, by contrast, acted as if he thought his mission was to *all* Israel rather than to some subset of Israel defined by one or more religious boundary markers (26.7). By fraternizing with tax collectors like Zaccheus, he indicated that outcasts were welcome in his movement. By preaching the good news so often and so directly to the poor, he lowered the social standards for entry into his movement. By teaching love for enemies, he included them in the groups to which his followers had a mission. By making a Samaritan a hero in a parable, he showed how far outside conventional bounds his thinking went, even outside Israel itself. "What amazes one again and again is the *inclusiveness* of Jesus' mission" (28.2).

This inclusiveness makes perfect sense if we understand the center of Jesus' ministry and the implications it had for Jews in general and Jesus' followers in particular. Here is the sequence:

1. Jesus announces and demonstrates the arrival of the reign of God

"The reign of God (*basileia tou Theou*) is undoubtedly central to Jesus' entire ministry. It is, likewise, central to his understanding of his own mission" (31.9).

Unlike his contemporaries, Jesus saw and declared the reign as arriving, not only as a future hope (32.2). This news electrified his hearers, and he did more than talk about it. He launched "an all-out attack on evil in all its manifestations" (32.9). Victims of disease, demon possession, calamities and ostracism were delivered (literally "saved") as he arrived among them (33.6).

2. The arriving reign of God pushes the Torah into second-place importance

If the arrival of God's reign is at the center of things, the Torah cannot be at the center any more. This shift at the center creates giant ripple effects throughout Jewish identity and the entire Jewish way of life. "The central place of the Torah in late Jewish apocalyptic is ... taken by the person and the cross of Christ. The place of life in the law is taken by fellowship with Christ in the following of the crucified one. The place of the self-preservation of the righteous from the world is taken by the mission of the believer in the world" (35.5, quoting Moltmann).

The defining mark of the reign of God arriving in Jesus is not pointing toward God's requirements as the Torah did. Rather it is love that startlingly reaches out beyond Israel and treats people as more important than the Torah's regulations (35.9). This love turns the Master into a servant who washes the feet of his followers (36.4).

3. Jesus reigns over his followers; he does not merely teach them as a rabbi

The first thing Jesus did after announcing the arrival of God's reign was to call his first four disciples (36.5). They are the ones who were given front-row seats to watch the arrival of the kingdom, get swept up into it, see how it worked, and pass it on. Following Jesus was drastically different from following other rabbis before or since (see Table 2 on p. 16).

4. Easter and Pentecost hit the world as the second and third waves of God's arriving reign

"It was the Easter experience that determined the early Christian community's self-definition and identity. Nothing else suffices to account for its coming into being" (40.2). "Intimately related to the resurrection, almost part of the Easter event itself, is the gift of the Spirit, which is equally integrally linked to mission" (40.7).

Jesus announced that God's reign was arriving, and he backed up the claim with his miracles, his teaching, and his formation of a group of followers. As if to say, "Oh, no, it is not coming," the powers of this world put him on the cross. As if to say, "Oh, yes, it is," God raised Jesus from the grave and, as the final blow, sent the Holy Spirit on his followers. As we will see later, the world

Table 2
Contrast of Rabbis and Jesus

Following a typical rabbi	Following Jesus
The follower chooses the rabbi	Jesus chooses his followers (37.1)
Authority is based on study of Torah	Jesus authorizes himself (37.5)
A student hopes to become a rabbi	A follower never moves up to a higher status (37.7)
Followers are students	Followers are students and servants (38.1)
A rabbi is a window into his teaching	Jesus' teaching is a window into himself (38.4)
A self-contained group of followers	The vanguard of the messianic people (39.2)

insisted, "Oh, no, it's not," by trying to stifle the disciples, but it was too late. The cross had breached the dam of the world's power. Through Easter and Pentecost the reign of God was pouring uncontrollably into the world, just as Jesus had predicted (40.9). The mission of Jesus' followers is to keep on witnessing to Easter, Pentecost, and (in faith) to his return.

Adding up the previous four points, we arrive at an inclusive gospel of the reign of God, good news for anyone and everyone who welcomes Jesus' message and centers his or her life on it. Note the importance of each person's response to this news. Jesus does not announce that people of all ethnic, social, and religious groups are already included in the reign of God, but that they are all eligible. The reign of God is "at hand" (Matt. 4:17) and people from any group may enter it by following him. Jesus did not teach social or ritual boundaries to mark the citizens of God's new reign/kingdom because he himself *was* the only boundary that mattered. The reign of God was like a bubble around him; getting into it and staying close to him amounted to the same thing.

THE CHURCH'S MISSION AFTER JESUS ASCENDED

Jesus concentrated his ministry on the people of Israel, and for a while after his resurrection and ascension, so did his followers. They saw themselves as one more theological camp within Judaism, along with the well-known camps of the

Pharisees, Sadducees, Essenes, and Zealots. Cutting across these theological categories was another very different criterion for categorizing Jews — the cultural and linguistic difference between the "Hebrews" (Aramaic-speaking Jews) and the "Hellenists" (Greek-speaking Jews, 42.7).

Within the group of Jews that followed Jesus, this cultural difference eventually proved decisive for its self-understanding and its mission, leading in about fifty years to the emergence of "Christianity" as a religion separate from Judaism. We need to take a closer look at the way this happened, for it was shaped by mission and has shaped mission ever since.

Not long after Jesus' ascension, the first decisive incident in this saga occurred in Jerusalem. Stephen, a high-profile Hellenist spokesman in the group of Jews that followed Jesus, was mobbed and stoned to death by the Jewish establishment, mostly Hebrews of the Sadducee group. They were defending Judaism against Stephen's criticisms, which they felt a "real" Jew (a Hebrew, not a second-class Hellenist Jew) would never have made. This sparked widespread attacks on the whole group of Jesus' followers, making Jerusalem unsafe for them.

Where to flee? Many headed for Antioch, which was the capital of the Roman provinces of Syria and Cilicia, and the third largest city in the Roman Empire at the time. " 'The largely anonymous, extraordinarily assured, open, active, pneumatic, city-oriented, Greek-speaking heirs of Stephen . . . ' exiled from Jerusalem, arrived there and founded a church made up of both Jews and Gentiles" (43.6, quoting Meyer). This Jew-Gentile combination, unlikely ever to happen among Jesus' followers in the Hebrew-dominated, homeland climate of Jerusalem, actually did happen in the highly cosmopolitan and progressive city of Antioch.

Once it became apparent that Gentiles could join the Antioch movement without becoming Jews by being circumcised, two things happened in short order. (1) The Jesus community acquired a new label, "Christians," by which the wider community was able to distinguish it from both "Jews" and "Gentiles." (2) The Hebrew leadership of the Jesus community in Jerusalem sent Barnabas to investigate.

At least from a human point of view, the whole future of the Jesus movement hung on Barnabas at this moment. What would he make of what the Hellenists were doing in Antioch? Would Jerusalem, home of the all-Hebrew apostles, tell Antioch it was out of bounds? Would Antioch accept the apostles' authority if they did so? Would the Hebrew followers of Jesus split from the Hellenistic ones?

The danger was real, but it was avoided. "Instead of censuring the Antiochians for what he saw, Barnabas was himself caught up in the events there and 'encouraged' the believers (Acts 11:23)" (43.8). Then he traveled to Tarsus to recruit Saul (Paul) to come to Antioch and help the Hellenists think through what they were doing. Paul was ideal for this role because he was something of a "Hebrew-Hellenist" himself, born and raised in Tarsus (a Greek-speaking setting, now in Turkey) but with long rabbinic schooling in Jerusalem. His encounter with Jesus on the road to Damascus had broken the authority of his schooling as a strict

Pharisee and forced him to do for his own sake the kind of rethinking of the Jewish heritage that the Hellenists at Antioch needed as they pioneered a Jew-Gentile community. We will return to this in the chapter on Paul's model of mission.

It should come as no surprise that Antioch was the place of the momentous decision by a group of Jesus' followers to become pro-active about sending missionaries to other countries, and that Paul and Barnabas were the first two sent (Acts 13:1–2). "This far-reaching decision and action was, however, not peripheral to the early Christian community, a kind of expendable extra. Rather, in retrospect it becomes clear 'that Christianity had never been more itself, more consistent with Jesus and more evidently en route to its own future, than in the launching of the world mission' " (44.4, quoting Meyer).

The success of the missionary work of Paul and Barnabas among Gentiles triggered further fears among the Hebrew group in Jerusalem, leading to the decisive "Apostolic Council" recorded in Acts 15, "by all odds the cardinal policy decision of the first-century church" (46.4, quoting Meyer). The door was opened for the Gentiles. Was it thereby closed for the Jews? That was certainly not the intent of the Hebrews who held the power in the Jesus movement in Jerusalem, but a completely different earthquake was about to hit Judaism and drastically alter their relationship to it.

The Jewish revolt against the Romans led to the destruction of Jerusalem in AD 70 and the banishment of all Jews from Jerusalem. This had quite different effects on the five subgroups of Judaism mentioned earlier. The Sadducees, whose power base was the Temple and all the Jerusalem power structures around it, quickly collapsed. The Zealots were killed or went underground. The Essenes, who had largely withdrawn to desert communities, gradually petered out. The Pharisees emerged as the defining center of "Judaism," no longer challenged by the other three groups. They were able to survive so well because their power base was in the local synagogues rather than the Temple and in the application of the Law of Moses to daily life, not only to Temple worship (46.5).

The strength of the Jesus movement, which by this time included large numbers of uncircumcised Gentiles, was not so directly affected by the destruction of Jerusalem. However, its identity was. It could no longer see itself as one of five (or more) sects within Judaism. It was one of only two left standing, and the other one hated it.

The Pharisees were convinced that God had allowed the destruction of Jerusalem because the Jews as a whole had not been faithful to the Law of Moses. The future restoration of Jerusalem would depend on keeping the Law more rigorously than ever. Since the Jesus movement appeared to be playing fast and loose with the Law of Moses, the Pharisees slammed the door on it. In AD 85 they made it official, prohibiting all "Nazarenes" (followers of Jesus of Nazareth) from attending synagogues (46.8).

Retracing the sequence, we see that Jesus' followers first saw themselves as a movement within Judaism, then recognized they had a mission to the Gentiles, then accepted that the Gentiles did not have to become subject to the Law of

Moses, then were excluded from Judaism by the Pharisees because they mixed with Gentiles. Thus Christianity became a new "religion" without intending to do so. Its emergence as a religion separate from Judaism was a byproduct of the theological implications of its mission to the Gentiles.

For much of its history, the church has "responded with anti-Jewishness to Judaism's anti-Christian stance" (52.2). The inability of the church "in the long run, to make Jews feel at home" is a sad theme running through the story of Christian mission after the first century (51.8).

THE MISSIONARY PRACTICE OF JESUS
AND THE EARLY CHURCH

Before looking more closely at the mission perspectives of Matthew, Luke, and Paul, let us summarize five of the main ingredients of the missionary ministry of Jesus and the early church.

1. A paradoxical and enigmatic announcement (47.1)

Jesus' mission did not appear as logical as the missions of many of his contemporaries. His ambiguous announcement of the "arriving" reign of God set him apart from those who pinned all their hopes on either the future or the present. He seemed to straddle the present and the future and to call others into the same strange position. Thus he had a lot of explaining to do about what he meant by the "reign of God."

2. A revolution with political implications (47.7)

On the surface the mission of Jesus and the early church did not appear to be political, but underneath, "It rejected all [Greek and Roman] gods and in doing this demolished the metaphysical foundations of prevailing political theories....Christians confessed Jesus as Lord of all lords — the most revolutionary political demonstration imaginable in the Roman Empire of the first centuries of the Christian era" (48.1).

3. A sociological innovation (48.3)

The combination of Jews and Gentiles, slave and free, rich and poor, cultured and uncultured into one new community was a "sociological impossibility" (48.3, quoting Hoekendijk). Humanly speaking, one could never get all those groups to identify with each other in one new social group. When the church achieved this, the Roman world took notice, even referring to the Christians as a "third race" (distinct from the "Greeks" and the "Jews"; 48.7).

4. A gentle sign of things to come (49.2)

Jesus and the early church understood that it was not their mission to impose the revolution of God's reign but only to signal it. They did not overthrow Rome; they only acted as if they knew of something and someone more powerful and important than Rome. They did not pressure Rome to legislate equality between Roman citizens and noncitizens; they showed the world what such equality looked like. They were gentle signs of things to come.

5. An acceptance of hostile reactions (49.7)

In this world the gentle sometimes become the trampled. Jesus and the early church accepted that as part of their mission. Jesus showed his followers how to deal with hostile reaction — just take it. Accept even death from your enemies, and if anyone tries to defend you violently, restrain him. Jesus and his followers were a sign of the times, but also, as Simeon said of the baby Jesus, "a sign that is spoken against" (49.7, quoting Luke 2:34). When the powers of Rome read the sign of Jesus and his followers, they thought it said, "Your days are numbered. A new regime is on the way." Such a placard is too threatening for politicians to tolerate, even if it is gently waved.

In sum, this is the description of a church on a mission: "A community of people who, in the face of the tribulations they encounter, keep their eyes steadfastly on the reign of God by praying for its coming, by being its disciples, by proclaiming its presence, by working for peace and justice in the midst of hatred and oppression, and by looking and working toward God's liberating future" (54.7).

YOUR VIEWS AND YOUR CONTEXT

4. New Testament mission is entirely based on three ideas that are central in the Old Testament but not in other religions or philosophies: (1) God steps into human history, (2) God makes promises about what he will do in history, and (3) God works through Israel to the nations. Are any of these missing from the worldview of the people you seek to evangelize? How does this absence make it difficult for these people to understand and accept the gospel of the arriving kingdom of Jesus, the Messiah?

5. Compare and contrast the following three common versions of the good news of Christianity with the good news as Jesus announced it in Matthew 4:17.

    (a) "Good news! I know how you can go to heaven when you die."

    (b) "Good news! I will teach you the moral principles for a life that pleases God."

    (c) "Good news! God is taking over now!"

6. Why did the Hebrew-speaking followers of Jesus in Jerusalem feel it was necessary to send Barnabas to investigate what the Greek-speaking (Hellenist) followers of Jesus were doing at Antioch? How did Barnabas's evaluation of the church at Antioch affect the whole church's view of its mission from then onward?

7. How closely does your church resemble the following description of the New Testament vision for the Christian community: "A community of people who, in the face of the tribulations they encounter, keep their eyes steadfastly on the reign of God by praying for its coming, by being its disciples, by proclaiming its presence, by working for peace and justice in the midst of hatred and oppression, and by looking and working toward God's liberating future" (54.7)?

8. How does the quotation above compare to a typical definition of the church one might find in an ecclesiology course or a systematic theology textbook? What do you conclude about theology and the church from the differences?

Chapter 2

Disciple-Making

Matthew's Model of Mission

(Bosch, TM, pp. 56–83)

Then Jesus came to them and said, "All authority in heaven and on earth has been given to me. Therefore go and make disciples of all nations, baptizing them in the name of the Father and of the Son and of the Holy Spirit, and teaching them to obey everything I have commanded you. And surely I am with you always, to the very end of the age."

(Matt. 28:18–20, NIV)[1]

This "Great Commission" is so often quoted in mission circles that it tends to take on a life of its own. "The 'Great Commission' is easily degraded to a mere slogan, or used as a pretext for what we have in advance decided [that 'mission' should mean]. . . . Matthew 28:18–20 has to be interpreted *against the background of Matthew's gospel as a whole*" (57.5).

What then does the Great Commission mean if we see it in its proper perspective as the text that draws together "all the threads woven into the fabric of Matthew" (57.5)? We will not know unless we consider first the community of people for whom Matthew wrote and the burning concerns of the place and time for which the Great Commission was originally designed.[2]

Matthew's purpose in writing was "to provide guidance to a community in crisis on how it should understand its calling and mission" (57.9). The community was probably a group of Jewish Christians who had moved out of Judea into a Gentile setting, possibly Syria. In the 70s or 80s AD (following the destruction of the Temple in Jerusalem), this community was facing an identity crisis: "Who are we? Are we really 'Jewish'? What are we doing here outside our homeland?

For a preview of the next three chapters, see the summary in Table 3 (p. 42).

1. All Scripture quotations are from the New International Version unless otherwise noted.

2. Bosch's doctorate was in New Testament, not mission, and his treatments of Matthew, Luke, and Paul demonstrate his ability to think like a New Testament scholar. By bridging the often yawning gap between New Testament studies and missiology, he makes a major contribution to both fields.

Do we have a mission to our fellow Jews? Do we have a mission to the Gentiles among whom we live now?"

In the midst of such questions, Matthew set out to write a gospel that is not merely a biography of Jesus with a missionary command conveniently tacked on at the end. Instead, from start to finish Matthew's Gospel is an attempt to help a community of Jesus-followers discover their new identity as Jews-with-a-mission or Jews-for-Gentiles. The discovery is rooted deeply in their Jewish heritage yet it enables them to engage the Gentile world not primarily as Jews but as messengers.

This new disciple-making identity is so paradoxical that Matthew appears almost self-contradictory when he describes it. At many points the story he tells seems very pro-Jewish (59.9):

- beginning the genealogy of Jesus with Abraham (1:1)

- mentioning that the disciples' first missionary assignment was restricted to Jews only (10:5)

- constantly quoting Jewish prophecies as if all his readers know and believe them (e.g., 27:9–10)

At other points the story sounds very pro-Gentile, such as in the wide range of Gentiles held up almost as heroes because they hail Jesus properly:

- the "wise men from the East" at his birth (2:1–12)

- the centurion who trusted Jesus to heal his servant with only a word (8:5–13)

- the Canaanite woman with the demon-possessed daughter (15:21–28)

- the centurion at the cross (27:54).

At the end of the day, Matthew calls on his readers to engage in mission to both Jews and Gentiles. To make disciples "of *all* nations" does not mean "of all Gentile nations." It means "of Jews and Gentiles alike" (64.5). From a Jewish perspective this implies a staggering redefinition of the identity of God's chosen people. Jews and Gentiles are placed on a par with each other before God and before Matthew's community. Something has happened in the light of which Jews and Gentiles look "alike"! What on earth could it be?

The arrival of the "kingdom" in Jesus has redefined everything. This earth-shaking fact is the beginning of Jesus' preaching (4:17), the constant theme of his teaching (e.g., chap. 13), and the basis and heart of the Great Commission (28:18–20). The arriving kingdom is a new cosmic reference point, the basis for all personal and group identity ever since Jesus announced it. Whoever is oriented to this point is transformed into a disciple and a missionary.

The word "kingdom" does not occur in the Great Commission but the idea clearly does in two ways. First, the often-overlooked basis for the Commission is a kingly statement, "All authority in heaven and on earth has been given to me. Therefore, go . . ." Jesus is saying, "Since I am now installed as king and *my kingdom is inaugurated,* go and make disciples...." Second, "teaching them to obey..." is in effect, "teaching them to live as *loyal subjects in my kingdom.*"

On the surface this may sound like our mission is to impose on the world a new law in the name of a new Moses (65.5). If we claim to announce a new kingdom and not a new legalism, what exactly is the difference between our mission of "teaching them to obey" and the teaching of rules? This is absolutely crucial for understanding mission according to Matthew.

1. First, the "teaching" that Matthew has in mind is neither indoctrination nor academic instruction. It is more what we would mean today by "shaping" or "formation." "Shaping them to obey all that I have commanded" (66.8).

2. All the "shaping" involved in our teaching is based on a deed, not an idea, a command, or an oracle. The deed is God's deed, sending the Messiah to announce and establish the kingdom. Our good news is the good news of the kingdom (4:23, 9:35). Our fundamental message is not, "Follow these rules," but "Come to terms with this wonderful God-deed."

3. The authority behind Jesus' commands was not the typical authority of Moses and the prophets, "God said so," but rather, "God is doing so." The teaching of Jesus about the central God-deed (the arrival of the kingdom) was proved by many deeds of Jesus (11:2).

4. To "obey" this deed-based teaching is the same as to reorient one's whole life to face these deeds or facts. Reorient means to turn, i.e., "repent" (4:17). Such reorientation does not mean "Come inside the fence marked off by these boundary rules," but "Turn your life around and walk out through the gate into a wide-open, new world of life." The goal is liberation, not forced conformity.

5. Getting reoriented to the ultimate God-deed is liberating because the ultimate God-deed is not a cold hard fact. It is a living, breathing fact — a person. "To encounter the kingdom is to encounter Jesus Christ" (71.1, quoting Senior and Stuhlmueller). If the center of our life is a person, not a law, the tone of our life cannot be legalistic. We are subjects of a king, not dehumanized objects who must have our goodness measured by some abstract standard.

6. Even though they are not oppressed into conformity, those who welcome the teaching about the kingdom really do "obey" and change. As they enter the reign/kingdom of God, the influence of God transforms them from the inside out. They are captivated, spellbound, overwhelmed by a force they just can't get enough of. They show a "righteousness" or "justice" higher than that of the Pharisees (5:20), yet they cannot claim to have achieved any of it by their own goodness (72.7).

7. When they obey, the followers of Jesus prove nothing about themselves and everything about Jesus. After all, could Jesus be a real "king" and rule a real "kingdom" if no one were obeying him? If Jesus' followers do not

obey him, the kingdom has not arrived and Jesus' announcement of it is a lie. Therefore his followers cannot dodge or explain away the ethical teachings of the Sermon on the Mount (chaps. 5–7), though that has often happened in church history. "Jesus actually expected all his followers to live according to these norms always and under all circumstances" (69.8).

If we understand the kind of teaching Matthew was talking about, we understand what he meant by a mission of "making disciples." The impact of this kind of "teaching" is discipleship, and a special kind of discipleship at that. When we receive and act upon the teaching of the reign/kingdom of God, we are not merely followers of a wise rabbi (teacher). We are followers of a king, one whose forefather is David, not Moses or Aaron (75.7). The necessary outcome of his teaching is discipleship, not churchmanship, that is, an internally transformed life made plain in everyday conduct, not an external conformity to a fixed pattern of religious practice.

The command to "make disciples" serves as the connecting bridge between the original circle of disciples and each successive generation of the ever-widening church on its mission. This means that all true disciples have an essentially missionary identity. "The followers of the earthly Jesus have to make others into what they themselves are: disciples" (74.4).

Weakness, suffering, and failure may still be facts of life for the disciples as they obey the Great Commission, just as they were for the disciples when Jesus was among them in person. However, the Great Commission is less a command reminding us how badly we are falling short than it is an empowerment creating what it requires, speaking it into being. "Jesus rules! Go let people know!" "Nobody who knows this can remain silent about it. He or she can do only one thing — help others also to acknowledge Jesus' lordship. And this is what mission is all about — 'the proclaiming of the lordship of Christ' " (78.6).

As we proclaim him, we testify not to his memory or his ideas but his presence. He is "God with us" (1:21, 28:20), the propeller of life-changing mission to the end of the age.

YOUR VIEWS AND YOUR CONTEXT

9. What does one realize about mission if the Great Commission (Matt. 28:18–20) is interpreted in relation to the whole of Matthew's Gospel instead of as an isolated quotation?

10. If Matthew has made a clear distinction between discipleship and legalism, how have so many churches and Christians missed it and become legalistic? What are they missing when they read Matthew?

11. How would Matthew's good news have had to change if Jesus had been a descendant of Moses or Aaron (tribe of Levi) rather than David (tribe of Judah)? What implications does this have for the common view that Jesus was primarily a good religious teacher?

Chapter 3

Transcending Class and Ethnicity

Luke's Model of Mission

(Bosch, TM, pp. 84–122)

"The Spirit of the Lord is on me, because he has anointed me to preach good news to the poor. He has sent me to proclaim freedom for the prisoners and recovery of sight for the blind, to release the oppressed, to proclaim the year of the Lord's favor." (Luke 4:18–19)

While it is true to say there is really only one mission described in the New Testament, it is also true that the one mission looks quite different when viewed from different angles. We have seen it from Matthew's angle. Now we turn to Luke (both the Gospel and Acts) and then to Paul in order to appreciate other dimensions of the complex reality of mission.

As we turn to Luke, we shall adopt the same approach we did with Matthew, looking at his key mission texts in the context of his entire work rather than isolating them as mission slogans. Reducing our mission thinking to a slogan is a real danger. Evangelicals have tended to use Matthew's Great Commission as their slogan and focus on individual conversions and church growth. On the other hand, ecumenicals generally and liberation theologians in particular have tended to use Luke 4:16–21 as their slogan (84.7) and focus on social transformation. Let us dig a little deeper into Luke's writings and see for ourselves what he is really saying.

In Luke 4 (quoted above), Jesus reads to his hometown synagogue from Isaiah 61 and then stuns his hearers by announcing that Isaiah's very down-to-earth messianic prophecy was fulfilled that day. Before they can recover from the first shock, he delivers a second one, implying that the messianic wonders would somehow come without God taking vengeance on the enemies of Israel as expected.[1] In fact, in this messianic kingdom God would bless outsiders, possibly

---

1. Jesus quit reading the text in the middle of a verse, omitting the phrase all his hearers knew by heart and cherished as their national hope, "...and the day of vengeance of our God" (Isa. 61:2; see 110.6).

even in preference to his own people Israel! (Luke 4:23–27). The crowd would not bear that reinterpretation of Isaiah's prophecy, and they almost killed Jesus for daring to suggest it (Luke 4:29–30).

Luke does more than suggest this idea. The theme runs right through his two-volume work (the Gospel and the book of Acts). *The good news is that God's vengeance on the nations has been suspended while God goes on an all-out mission of gracious forgiveness, inviting outsiders to seats of honor at the messianic banquet table* (108.5).

Before we examine Luke's Gospel and his view of mission in more detail, we need to consider his audience. It appears he, a Gentile, was writing primarily to Gentile Christians in the decade of the 80s, that is, after the destruction of Jerusalem by the Romans. Jesus had not returned in the lifetime of the apostles, as had been widely expected. Gentile Christians were facing questions such as, "Who are we really? How do we relate to the Jewish past? Is Christianity a new religion? And above all, how do we relate to the earthly Jesus, who is gradually and irrevocably receding into the past?" (85.9).

As a historian and a theologian, Luke answers these questions by helping the Christians of his day see their lives as one stage in the flow of God's activity in the world — past, present, and future. They were in continuity with previous stages but they also had a present missionary identity because they could foresee the stage God was bringing into being. They were both the product of mission and the bearers of mission. They were like iron filings that under the influence of a magnet had become magnetic themselves. We can understand their magnetism and their mission by examining three of their key questions.

WHO ARE WE?

We Christians are the multiethnic, multiclass community that came into being because God suspended his vengeance on all nations and sent his deliverer to Israel. Our community is an anomaly among the nations of the earth because of the way it transcends social class and ethnic identity. We need to understand both how this leveling of class and race works among us and what message it sends to the world.

How class and ethnicity are leveled by the good news

Every key aspect of Luke's missiology has a leveling or boundary-transcending effect.

- There is only one Messiah for all the nations (Acts 1:8).

- Repentance and forgiveness are the same route to the same salvation regardless of ethnicity or class (Luke 24:47).

- The Holy Spirit is poured out in the same way on young and old, male and female, Jew and Gentile (Acts 2:17–18, 10:44–45).

- The coming messianic banquet (Luke 13:28–30) may be the greatest leveler of all, where people of all classes and nations sit down to eat and celebrate together. With this feast as the envisioned end of mission and history, the familiar human dividing lines of class and race are transcended. They simply cannot mean very much any more.

The leveling theme jumps out at the reader constantly in both the Gospel, where economic class is the main barrier to overcome, and Acts, where ethnicity is the hurdle. Let us look more closely at both.

The Gospel of Luke is preoccupied with "the poor," that is, "all who experience misery" (99.3). We have already seen this in Jesus' announcement in Luke 4:18, the "good news for the poor." Many other passages stress this theme of God's love for the poor and his plan to turn the tables on the rich (1:53, 3:10–14, 6:20 and 24, 12:16–21, 16:19–31, 19:1–10; see 98.3–99.4).

Unlike many who (mis)quote him, Luke does not conclude that a pro-poor gospel must be anti-rich. In fact, Luke has even been called the "evangelist of the rich" (101.8), not in the sense that he makes the way easy for them but that he deliberately addresses them as a redeemable group. He "wants the rich and respected to be reconciled to the message and way of life of Jesus and the disciples; he wants to motivate them to a conversion that is in keeping with the social message of Jesus" (101.9, quoting Schotroff and Stegemann). Zaccheus (Luke 19:1–10), Barnabas (Acts 4:36–37), Lydia (Acts 16:13–15), and others in Luke's writings are model converts among the rich.

As the Gospel of Luke emphasizes the poor, the book of Acts emphasizes the Gentiles. Nothing can be clearer from Pentecost than the fact that God was on a mission to make his message known to people of all ethnic groups. Taking the initiative by his own grace, he would go so far as to miraculously enable his witnesses to speak the languages of those groups rather than require them to learn the language of his people. This transcending of the language barrier is the defining miracle and symbol marking the launch of the church on God's mission, and it is the defining theme of the book of Acts.

The stories of Peter at the home of Cornelius (Acts 10:23–48) and the "Jerusalem Council" (Acts 15:1–21) are exactly on the same point. Did God intend for Gentiles to become part of his own people, and if so, would they need to come under the Law of Moses, which had been the defining boundary of the Jewish people? By now we should realize that in Luke's view, the only purposes of boundaries and fences were to climb on or jump over. And since the Jew-Gentile distinction was the most important boundary (ethnic, cultural, and theological) to Jews of that day, when it was relativized by the Jerusalem Council all other boundaries lost their absolute quality too. The one remaining definitive absolute was the Messiah, the Jewish Messiah who was and is the hope of all the nations. If the Messiah is among us, all other fences are down.

What the existence of a multiethnic, multiclass church says to the world

Since boundary maintenance is a main preoccupation of all human groups, the existence of a boundary-transcending group is an anomaly. It will catch people by surprise, attract attention and demand an explanation. What is going on here? How is this possible? The explanation can only be Jesus, the Holy Spirit, and forgiveness, that is, the gospel. In other words, just by being itself as the Messiah-centered, multiethnic, multiclass community, the church raises the question to which the good news of Jesus is the answer.

This is what lies behind the phrase "You will be my witnesses" (Acts 1:8). The Messiah unites people of all classes and races in a way that no other force can. Their unity is a testimony to his power and presence. If there is a church of this united kind, there must be a Messiah, a defining center more important than any social dividing line.

HOW ARE WE RELATED TO JEWS?

It would have been easy and perhaps logical for Luke to present a gospel in which the Jewish features were neglected or even removed in order not to create problems for Gentiles who wanted to become Christians. As we have said, Luke was not Jewish himself. But what Luke actually did was stress the continuity between the Jews of the previous era and the multiethnic church of the new era (94.6).

For example, Luke does not describe the church as a "new Israel" (96.8). We are rather part of the old Israel, which has regrettably split down the middle over Jesus and his good news of God's suspended vengeance (96.4). If we see Luke's point, we can never let the church become a new Gentile group of privileged insiders who look down on the Jews as outsiders. To do so would be to fall back into the very error the Messiah came to remove!

Luke is therefore careful not to bash the Jews. His criticisms of the Pharisees are mild compared to Matthew's blasts at them (92.5). His theology is so focused on Jerusalem that it looks like a Jew wrote it (93.6). In fact, "he has an exceptionally positive attitude to the Jewish people, their religion and their culture" (92.3). He goes to great lengths in chapters 1 and 2 to connect the birth of Jesus to Jewish prophecies about a Jewish messiah who would save Israel.

Here we come to the heart of the matter. For Luke, the Messiah is the hinge who connects the Gentile door to the Jewish doorframe. And this is the great offense for many Jews. They thought the arrival of the Messiah would be the day the filthy, oppressive Gentile door would be smashed and torched, not the day it would be salvaged and hinged to them! They would rather separate themselves from the Messiah than let the Messiah connect Gentiles to them.

HOW ARE WE RELATED TO JESUS?

Jesus had not been physically present on the earth for perhaps fifty years by the time Luke wrote. Very few still alive had ever seen Jesus. The connection of personal memory would soon be gone. What sort of connection would replace it? Only one of second-hand witness, written records and oral teaching?

Luke presents the Holy Spirit as our ever-present dynamic connection with the risen, ascended, and ruling Messiah. "The same Spirit in whose power Jesus went to Galilee also thrusts the disciples into mission. The Spirit becomes the catalyst, the guiding and driving force of mission" (113.8).

The Spirit is so central to mission that Jesus commands his followers not to begin their mission until he sends the Spirit on them. We might imagine they could have at least made a start on their own. After all, they knew Jesus' teaching and had seen his resurrection with their own eyes. They had plenty to teach and plenty to report. But Jesus forbade them to go anywhere until they were "clothed with power from on high"! (Luke 24:48).

This prohibition shows us how Jesus regarded his first batch of missionaries. Their mission was not primarily to spread his teaching or even to attest his resurrection. It was to do those things while showing the world that the same Holy Spirit who had descended on him at his baptism was living in them now.

In other words, Jesus himself was not really gone, nor was he present only in their memory. He was present by his Spirit. Matthew's Great Commission had said, "I am with you always" (Matt. 28:20). Luke explains how that idea was and is fleshed out by the Spirit, incarnated in the believers. They are not merely human eyewitnesses; they were bearers of God's mission, corroborated by God's power. Hence Luke's second volume is titled the "Acts" of the apostles, not the "Teaching" of the apostles or even the "Witness" of the apostles.

Since we have that ongoing connection with Christ, the "Great Commission" from Luke's perspective is more a promise than a command (114.1). It is a description of what is bound to happen once the Spirit enters the disciples. They go on a mission not as "men who, being what they were, strove to obey the last orders of a beloved Master, but [as] men who, receiving a Spirit, were driven by that Spirit to act in accordance with the nature of that Spirit" (114.2, quoting Allen).

THE ONE REMAINING BOUNDARY

We might suppose that if all boundaries are transcended, all humanity is now included in God's multiethnic, multiclass people and all are at peace with God. At last we can quit talking about God's judgment and quit thinking in terms of "saved" and "lost." But such a view cuts the nerve of Luke's idea of mission. "There can be no doubt that 'salvation' as well as its attendant ideas of repentance and forgiveness of sins, are central to Luke's two-volume work" (104.9).

How can Luke, the boundary transcender, still insist on a strict boundary between repentant and unrepentant, forgiven and unforgiven, saved and lost? How can a writer so full of such mercy and grace also record so many instances of people who were not forgiven (such as the rich young ruler, Luke 18:23) and were even cursed with blindness (Elymas the sorcerer, Acts 13:8–11) or eaten up by parasites (Herod, Acts 12:21–23)?

This makes sense if we realize that the gospel of Jesus does not mean that all boundaries are gone. It means that only one boundary is left with any meaning — the boundary between those who "repent" (reorient themselves to face and welcome the Messiah) and the others. But the meaning of even this last boundary is different from the meaning of all other ethnic and class boundaries. Those inside the Messiah boundary are not to defend it but to cross it in mission. They are not to use the boundary to keep the outsiders out. Rather they are to go out across the boundary and bring in as many as they can (Luke 14:21–23).

"The Jesus Luke introduces to his readers is somebody who brings the outsider, the stranger, and the enemy home and gives him and her, to the chagrin of the 'righteous,' a place of honor at the banquet in the reign of God" (108.5). The so-called "righteous" are those who want to defend the boundary and let the outsiders get the judgment they deserve. Jesus wants to cross the boundary in grace and bring the outsiders in to a feast they do not deserve. Thus Jesus and the "righteous" are at cross-purposes, while Jesus and repentant sinners of all classes and nations (including Jews) are on their way to enjoying a meal together. Luke, the Gentile, will be at the table, loving every minute of it.

YOUR VIEWS AND YOUR CONTEXT

12. Suppose that Jesus' announcement of the good news was written this way in the New Testament: "The Spirit of the Lord is on me, and I have good news for everyone — rich or poor, powerful or oppressed, healthy or sick, Jew or Gentile, black or white." Would the gospel as you preach it fit better with that statement than with the real statement in Luke 4:18–19, which seems to favor the poor, the blind, and the oppressed? Discuss briefly.

13. Suppose you explain to a non-Christian friend Luke's view of the church as a community that transcends social and ethnic divisions. The friend observes, "But the churches I know are divided along social and ethnic lines. How is this possible? Don't they read Luke and Acts?" What would you say to that friend?

14. In the flow of the story of mission in Luke and Acts, what was the significance of the pouring out of the Holy Spirit on the church? How would the story have changed if this had not happened?

15. Compare and contrast Matthew's model of mission with Luke's. What do they have in common? How do the identities of the authors and their audiences affect the slant of what they wrote?

Chapter 4

Making the Most of the Grace Period

Paul's Model of Mission

(Bosch, TM, pp. 123–78)

Paul, an apostle — sent not from men nor by man, but by Jesus Christ and God the Father, who raised him from the dead — and all the brothers with me, To the churches in Galatia: Grace and peace to you from God our Father and the Lord Jesus Christ, who gave himself for our sins to rescue us from the present evil age, according to the will of our God and Father, to whom be glory for ever and ever. Amen. (Gal. 1:1–5)

As we considered the mission texts of Matthew and Luke in light of the entire flow of their writings, so we will consider Paul's views. Mission so permeates Paul's thinking that it is hard to identify any parts of his writing that could not rightly be called "mission texts."[1]

The reasons are clear. Paul was a missionary — a person specially called and sent — from day one of his Christian experience (127.2), when his encounter with Jesus the Messiah on the road to Damascus caused the most dramatic U-turn ever made by a traveler (Acts 9:1–19). All his letters now in our Bibles were written either to churches that were mission outposts he pioneered or to individuals connected with his mission in some way. All his theology is "missionary theology" (124.7).

---

1. As the basis for his description of Paul's model of mission, Bosch has voluntarily restricted himself to Paul's letters rather than the descriptions in Acts. He has even kept to only the seven letters most widely accepted as genuinely Pauline (Romans, 1 and 2 Corinthians, Galatians, Philippians, 1 Thessalonians, and Philemon). Those, he says, are more than enough to try to handle in one chapter (123.9).

Since his chapter is fifty-six pages and my treatment is only eight pages, I must caution the reader against trusting my summary too much. It is done in very broad strokes, accurate as far as it goes but lacking in many important details and nuances. Even Bosch remarks of his own chapter, "Paul's thinking, truth to tell, is so complex that, at the end of a reflection like this, one has the distinct feeling of still standing only at the beginning" (170.4). That is ten times truer of my summary.

THE COSMIC GRACE PERIOD[2]

If Matthew's view of mission is disciple-centered and Luke's is boundary-centered, Paul's is time-centered. Paul is supremely conscious of the fact that through Jesus Christ, God the Father has inaugurated a cosmic grace period, a suspension of his judgment for a set time. (See "The Law of Moses" section beginning on p. 35.) Paul's mission is to urge the nations to understand the meaning of this grace period and take advantage of it for the purpose God intended before it runs out.

Paul can readily understand and excitedly preach a cosmic grace period because he has experienced it in microcosm in his own life. He was an enemy of the followers of Christ, but God by his own gracious choice intervened, turned Paul around, and gave him a new mission in life — to preach Jesus to the nations. "For Paul, then, the most elemental reason for proclaiming the gospel to all is not just his concern for the lost, nor is it primarily the sense of an obligation laid upon him, but rather a sense of *privilege*" (138.5, cf. Rom. 1:5, 15:5). Granted a personal grace period, he is overwhelmed with gratitude, which he expresses by spreading the news of the cosmic grace period (138.7). Given a divine calling, he calls others.

Let us look a bit closer at the concept of a grace period, a set time during which a debtor is not penalized for not paying a debt that has come due. The creditor unilaterally decides whether to give a grace period and if so, for how long. A debtor can do nothing to earn a grace period. At the end of the period, the debtor is required to pay the amount that was due at the beginning — no more, no less.

The cosmic grace period is similar in that God decided unilaterally to give humanity a grace period. The sins of our race came to a climax with the rejection and execution of Jesus, the central figure in God's plan to establish his visible reign on earth. We humans should have had to pay for our crime right then, and pay with our lives, for we had taken a life in our murderous attempt to block God's cosmic plan.

Instead of making us pay then and there, God gave humanity a grace period. He postponed the day of our judgment. This is good news, but Paul has even more to reveal. If we make proper use of the grace period, responding to it as our Creditor desires, we can have our debt canceled altogether. When the grace period ends, we will owe nothing! How is this possible? What is the secret to having our debt erased? Paul's whole mission and his many explanations of the good news all answer this question, but none of the explanations will make sense unless we first understand that we are living in a period between the Messiah's death and resurrection and the Messiah's return. We must orient our lives to these two realities that mark the beginning and the end of the grace period.

2. The "grace period" analogy is not used by Bosch. It is added here as an attempt to draw together several of the main threads of Paul's thought as Bosch has outlined them, especially apocalyptic, the Law, and eschatology.

Figure 1
Two Views of the Messiah's Arrival

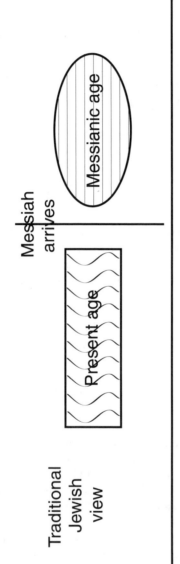
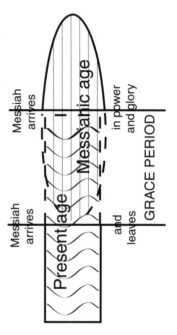

Traditional Jewish view

Present age

Messiah arrives

Messianic age

Paul's discovery

Present age

Messiah arrives

Messiah arrives and leaves

Messianic age

Messiah arrives in power and glory

GRACE PERIOD

THE LAW OF MOSES
AND THE MESSIAH OF GOD

To understand why Paul is so struck by the grace period and so driven to explain his discovery to the whole world, we must realize how novel this concept was to someone schooled (as he probably was) in the Jewish apocalyptic tradition (140.1, 161.6). According to that tradition, God had set a time for executing judgment on the world using the standards of the Law of Moses, which defined the boundaries of God's covenant people. On the appointed Judgment Day, God and his Messiah would strike the nations outside the covenant with sudden, overwhelming power and sweep them away, delivering his people from their oppression, idolatry, and wickedness forever.

"Paul struggles with the problem that although the Messiah has come, his kingdom has not" (142.9). Instead of doing what the Jews expected, God has split the messianic arrival into two parts, inserting a completely unexpected grace period between them as shown in Figure 1 (p. 34).

The grace period changes everything. We are now living in two overlapping ages, as shown by the overlapping lines in Figure 1. The key to living in this time is to understand the new standard by which the world will be judged when the apocalypse finally does arrive as expected. Judgment will not depend on being inside or outside the Law but inside or outside the Messiah. As people used to be judged by how they responded to God's gift of the Law, so now they will be judged by how they respond to God's greater gift, the Messiah. If the Law of Moses was the ace of all religious systems, the Messiah's arrival trumped it. That is why being "in Christ" (i.e., "in the Messiah") is such a common theme in Paul's writings (e.g., Rom. 8:9, 12:5, 1 Cor. 15:22, Gal. 3:28, Phil. 1:1). Everything depends on it.

Of course, one must be sure that this Jesus whom Paul preaches is the real Messiah, and to do that, one must get around the very public fact that he died. Paul gets around it in two ways. First, he makes sense of the death by describing it not as the derailing of God's plan but as the perfect sacrifice God uses to take the plan to a whole new level. "His substitutionary death on the cross, and that alone, has opened the way to reconciliation with God" (158.7, cf. 2 Cor. 5:18–21). Second, Paul pins his entire life and message on the reports of Jesus' literal resurrection. "If only for this life we have hope in Christ, we are to be pitied more than all men" (1 Cor. 15:19).

MEGACHANGES

This central change from Law to Messiah brings other massive changes with it. Paul's mission and his writings may be viewed as attempts to spell out these changes against the backdrop of Jewish apocalyptic thinking of his day.

The distinction between insiders and outsiders

In Jewish apocalyptic there were clear-cut distinctions between light and darkness, good and evil, insiders and outsiders. If the standard of judgment on the Day of the Lord will be response to the crucified and risen Messiah rather than response to the Law of Moses, then the distinction between Jewish insiders and Gentile outsiders (which used to mean everything) means nothing at all any more.

Paul demands agreement about this, especially in Galatians. If people compromise on this point, they undo the meaning of their own baptism and compromise the core of the gospel itself (167.2). The same is true for differences of class and sex (Gal. 3:27). "In a very real sense mission, in Paul's understanding, is saying to people from all backgrounds, 'Welcome to the new community, in which all [whether former insiders or former outsiders] are members of one family and bound together by love' " (168.3).

The distinction between this age and the messianic age

Jewish apocalyptic maintained a black and white distinction between the current dismally corrupt, oppressive age and the glorious age that would begin with the Messiah's arrival. Paul now sees that these ages overlap in the grace period between the two comings of the Messiah. Christians are those who recognize and welcome the Messiah today, thus putting one foot into the messianic age already. What will be true of the whole world in the messianic age is already partly true of Christians.

"The church is . . . the sign of the dawning of the new age in the midst of the old, and as such the vanguard of God's new world. It is simultaneously acting as pledge of the sure hope of the world's transformation at the time of God's final triumph and straining itself in all its activities to prepare the world for its coming destiny" (169.8).

The relationship between God's covenant people and the world

In Jewish apocalyptic, God's people are under attack by evil forces of this world and therefore eagerly waiting to be rescued by the Messiah. The hostile world is a complete write-off from that perspective. But as Paul describes things, God's people see that the grace period means there is real hope for the nations, even those who have oppressed God's people until now. Instead of waiting for the nations to receive the blistering annihilation they so richly deserve, God's people now have a mission to them, calling them to glorify God.

How will the church get the nations to listen? Mostly by being itself, that is, by being an exhibit of God's new creation in Christ (168.7). As such, the church cannot help being noticed. It sticks out among the nations like a goose would stick out in the flock if it started growing the wings of an eagle. The two eagle wings the church is growing are its initiative toward the world and its response to the world's persecution.

When taking the initiative, the church engages with the world in many ways, serving compassionately, treating people with the justice and peace that will be typical of life in the coming messianic age. God's (eagle) people are " 'missionary by their very nature,' through their unity, mutual love, exemplary conduct, and radiant joy" (168.9).

The church recognizes clearly that these fine initiatives are out of step with the world's "oppressive structures of the powers of sin and death. . . . As agitators for God's coming reign; [God's people] must erect, in the here and now and in the teeth of those structures, signs of God's new world" (176.8). The world's powers will certainly react and the church will certainly suffer but it will not respond to suffering as the Jews did. Instead, it will see suffering is "a mode of missionary involvement" in the world. God's people on a mission are sharing in the suffering of Christ for the sake of the world's redemption (177.6). The church is above all a sign of grace, and what clearer sign could there be than to accept suffering as Christ accepted it on the cross?

No apocalypticist had that outlook on either suffering or the world that inflicted it. They all wanted the Messiah to come, their own suffering to end, and the suffering of their persecutors to begin. Paul could no longer see the world in those terms.

Why all the changes could happen

The changes Paul describes are too radical and real to be brought about merely by a change of religious perspective or a new "law" brought by Jesus. They can only occur if some new spiritual power has become available, a power neither Jews nor Gentiles had ever had, a power no apocalypticist had dreamed possible for humans in the present age. According to Paul, this is exactly what has happened.

"For what the law was powerless to do in that it was weakened by the sinful nature, God did by sending his own Son in the likeness of sinful man to be a sin offering. . . . You, however, are controlled not by the sinful nature but by the Spirit, if the Spirit of God lives in you. And if anyone does not have the Spirit of Christ, he does not belong to Christ" (Rom. 8:3, 9).

The Law of Moses had pointed the way, but we humans could never get there. We always strayed or stumbled. The Spirit now picks us up, dusts us off, and carries us to the destination. To be "in Christ" (Paul's favorite phrase) is to have this powerful, transforming Spirit within as part of us.

To be under the control of the Spirit of Christ is to be under the control of Christ himself. This is what it means to enter the "kingdom" (or control) of the Messiah. "For the kingdom of God is not a matter of eating and drinking [according to the Law of Moses], but of righteousness, peace and joy in the Holy Spirit" (Rom. 14:17).

In other words, by the Spirit at work in the church, God is creating a new community made up of a new kind of human being so the world can have a sneak preview of life in the age to come. "If anyone is in Christ, he is a new creation; the old has gone, the new has come!" (2 Cor. 5:17). "This evidence of the Spirit's active presence guarantees for Paul that the messianic age had dawned" (144.2).

PAUL'S MISSION AND STYLE

This message of transformed apocalyptic is the message that Paul absolutely has to get out to the world at any cost. "He is charged with enlarging in this world the domain of God's coming world" (150.8). He wants to make the most of God's grace period, which means he wants others to make the most of it too. How does he go about this? Totally under the influence of the Spirit of Christ, that is, graciously, urgently, strategically, with the confidence of a man who knows he cannot lose.

1. Graciously

As the Messiah in his first coming to earth did not impose his rule on anyone, so Paul, his ambassador, does not badger anyone into putting faith in the Messiah. "Paul's missionary message is not a negative one.... He does proclaim the wrath of God, but only as the dark foil of an eminently positive message — that God has already come to us in his Son and will come again in glory" (147.9). Paul reasons with people. He appeals. He pleads (2 Cor. 5:20). He graciously presents the message of grace.

This is Paul's grace-filled message: "the proclamation of a new state of affairs that God has initiated in Christ, one that concerns the nations and all of creation and that climaxes in the celebration of God's final glory" (148.3). But the new state of affairs does not come about automatically. "People have to 'transfer' from the old reality to the new by an act of belief and commitment" (149.1), that is, by the act of confessing that Jesus is Lord of all. "The taproot of Paul's cosmic understanding of mission is a personal belief in Jesus Christ, crucified and risen, as Savior of the world" (178.5).

Those who trust Jesus as Messiah are "justified through faith" (Rom. 5:1), that is, already set right before God and adopted into the community that through the Spirit is gearing up for the messianic age. Their debt is canceled because they have renounced the human decision to crucify Jesus, which was what plunged the human race far deeper into debt than we had ever been.

To use a different image, it is as if these justified people have inhaled or absorbed the grace that God has injected into the world's atmosphere through the death of Christ. At the end of the grace period God will take grace out of the atmosphere but the grace they have absorbed will preserve them.

Paul is passionate but never belligerent about explaining this "inhale-the-grace" message. Jesus Christ makes so much sense to him that he believes many others who hear the good news will put their faith in Christ, as they have graciously been destined to do. All they need is a clear picture of God's gracious plan, long kept secret but now revealed in Christ for the duration of the grace period.

2. *Urgently*

Paul's mission is greatly affected by one decisive difference between ordinary grace periods and this God-given one — we, the debtors, have not been told how long the grace period will last. Though Paul does not go into much detail about what bad things will happen at the end of the grace period (148.7), he knows that when the grace period ends, grace ends. The mission is therefore urgent. Like soccer players in a game where regulation time has expired, we do not know exactly how much "injury time" the referee is adding on. Only the referee knows. When he blows his whistle, that's it. No more goals can be scored.

This sense of urgency in mission is another sharp contrast between Paul's writings and ordinary apocalyptic. Rather than looking forward (perhaps even with a sense of satisfaction) to the final whistle on the day when the Messiah will execute justice on the wicked, Paul wants to do all he can to reduce the number of wicked who will be punished on that day.

3. *Strategically*

Urgency calls for strategy, not frantic spurts of mission. Paul is strategic both at the theoretical and practical levels of mission.

On the theoretical level, God's grace period is divided into two phases. In the first phase the good news of the Messiah whom the Jews rejected will be spread to the nations and they will welcome him as the Lord of all the earth. In the second phase the Jews, seeing the Gentiles flock to the Messiah, will become jealous of the way God is blessing the Gentiles. Then they themselves will turn to Jesus, the Messiah they rejected before the grace period started. Together Jews and Gentiles will enter a renewed world and cosmos under the Messiah's reign.

This wildly creative plan of God is explained in the heart of Romans (chapters 9–11), which is the letter regarded as the heart of all Paul's teaching. By no stretch of the imagination does Paul's missionary strategy abandon the Jews. In fact, "It is Paul's fundamental conviction that the destiny of all humankind will be decided by what happens to Israel" (159.7). Paul is concentrating on Gentile evangelization but still has the Jews in mind. He believes that success of the gospel among the Gentiles (phase 1) will create the conditions that will almost automatically bring on phase 2, Jewish conversion.

Putting this theory into practice, Paul concentrates his mission efforts "on the district or provincial capitals [such as Philippi, Thessalonica, Corinth, and

Ephesus], each of which stands for a whole region. . . . In each of these he lays
the foundations for a Christian community, clearly in the hope that, from these
strategic centers, the gospel will be carried into the surrounding countryside and
towns" before it is too late (130.2).

4. Confidently

Paul is dead sure of three things: the Messiah was here, the Messiah will be
back, and in the meantime he is here among us by his Spirit. None of these
depend on human design, human activity, or human timing. God has set things
in motion and God is the timekeeper.

One thing God set in motion was Paul's mission. As we noted in the quote
at the beginning of this chapter, Paul was an apostle, "sent not from men nor by
man, but by Jesus Christ and God the Father" (Gal. 1:1). There is no stopping
such a person. He and his colleagues are "afflicted — not crushed; perplexed —
not despairing; persecuted — not forsaken; struck down — not destroyed" (177.6,
see 2 Cor. 4:8f).

"Lesslie Newbigin suggests that nowhere in the New Testament is the essential character of the church's mission set out more clearly than in the passage
[referred to] above (2 Cor. 4:7–10). 'It ought to be seen,' he says, 'as the classic
definition of mission' " (145.4). Mission at its heart involves the conflict between
the message of the messianic future and the forces of the anti-messianic present,
the same "present" that put Jesus on the cross when the grace period began.

The world with all its might keeps trying to extinguish the witness of the messianic age, but those very efforts only enlarge and deepen the witness by showing
the incredible resilience of the messengers. The world has not extinguished the
witness but rather exhausted its own resources in the attempt. Now the only thing
that can happen — must happen, will happen — is the collapse of the world and
the triumph of God.

YOUR VIEWS AND YOUR CONTEXT

16. The analogy of the grace period is not in Bosch's book. It has been
    added as an explanatory aid. What do you consider to be the strengths
    and weaknesses of this analogy?

17. Paul presents Jesus as being incredibly important because his life, death,
    and resurrection brought about a change from one historical period (the
    age of the Law of Moses) to the next (the cosmic grace period). However,
    many ethnic groups and religions do not attach much importance to the dis-
    tinctions between any historical periods. Is Paul's message then irrelevant
    to them? Is Jesus irrelevant? If not, how can the relevance be explained?

18. Agree or disagree with the following statement: *The three changes from a
    Jewish apocalyptic worldview to a Christian worldview (insider–outsider,*

*present age–messianic age, defensive–missionary) are so interwoven that
if any one of them is true, the other two must also be true.* Briefly explain
your reasons.

19. Identify at least five themes mentioned in Galatians 1:1–5 and explain how
    they are woven together in Paul's theology of mission.

20. Which of the four aspects of Paul's style of mission (gracious, urgent,
    strategic, confident) do you think is least evident in the church as it goes
    about its mission in your country or region today? What problems does this
    cause? Write a paragraph that Paul might write on this subject if he came
    for a visit.

21. Based on the summary table of New Testament models of mission (Table 3,
    p. 42), do you consider the mission perspective of Matthew, Luke, or Paul
    to be the most appropriate framework for mission in your context? What
    definition of mission are you using to evaluate their appropriateness?

22. In the bottom line of Table 3, which emphases shared by Matthew, Luke,
    and Paul are not shared by your church in a very noticeable way? To
    what extent do you share in the responsibility to do something about that
    discrepancy?

23. Write a prayer based on one or more of the ideas represented in the bottom
    half of Figure 1 (the Messiah's arrival, p. 34).

Table 3
Summary of Some New Testament Models of Mission

	Self-understanding of author and audience	Focus	Key concept	Key text	Mission
Matthew	A disciple helping other Jewish disciples widen their mission beyond Judaism	Discipleship	Kingdom of God	Mt. 28:18-20	Carry the good news
Luke-Acts	A former outsider (Gentile) helping God's new inter-ethnic community understand its identity and mission	Transcending boundaries	Holy Spirit	Lk. 4:18-19	Go with the Spirit
Paul	A Jewish persecutor turned apostle helping Jew and Gentile converts of his mission understand their conversion	Time (grace period)	Salvation	Gal. 1:1-5	Seize the day
In common	Mission is the core of who we are, not an incidental matter. We have to adapt our mission as our situation changes.	God's new action in the Messiah calls for a new response from everyone.	God's liberating influence is arriving among us with present and eternal implications.	God sent Jesus and he sends his messengers.	Be proactive. Tell the whole world about the Messiah.

PART TWO

PARADIGMS
IN CHURCH HISTORY

Chapter 5

The Concept of Paradigm Change in Church History

(Bosch, TM, pp. 181–89)

Having surveyed three of the main strands of New Testament theology of mission, we may be tempted to jump straight to some conclusions for our day (189.6). If we yield to that temptation, some of our conclusions will probably be wrong because we will not be adequately aware of the way our own era and culture limit our capacity to interpret God's revelation. "It is an illusion to believe that we can penetrate to a pure gospel unaffected by any cultural and other human accretions" (182.6).

The way to cope with our cultural limitations is to become aware of them, which is tricky because they are like dirt on the back of our clothing. We cannot see them without a mirror. The mirror we need to look into is history. By seeing how several other historical eras limited and shaped the Christians of those times, we may be able to recognize our own limitations better. If we know who Christians thought they were in other eras, we may understand better who we are today as God's people in mission (183.8). Then as faithful disciples we will be able to apply the New Testament more properly and "prolong the logic of the ministry of Jesus and the early church in an imaginative and creative way to our own time and context" (181.6) rather than build a culture-bound theology of mission around a few favorite mission texts.

We will follow Hans Küng's outline of six major periods in Christian history, each with its own theological framework and its own understanding of mission — the New Testament period, the patristic period, the medieval Roman Catholic period, the Protestant Reformation, the Enlightenment, and the period now dawning (181.9).[1] Each period has a "general frame of reference" or paradigm which to a large extent molds the "faith, experiences, and thought processes" of everyone living in that time (183.2).

---

1. For a more nuanced approach to breaking church and mission history into periods, see Stephen Bevans and Roger Schroeder, *Constants in Context* (Maryknoll, N.Y.: Orbis Books, 2004).

Figure 2
How Human Progress Occurs

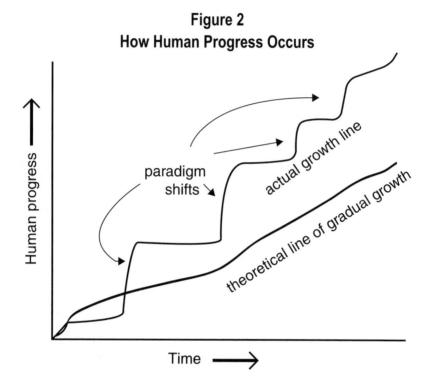

Paradigm theory, popularized a generation ago by the physicist Thomas Kuhn, argues that science does not grow in small gradual steps but in quick bursts that are no less than "revolutions," as shown in Figure 2 (184.4). These occur as a small group of people realizes that something is fundamentally wrong with the paradigm that everyone in their field of science has accepted for a long time. For example, Einstein thought there was something fundamentally wrong with the theory that matter and energy were two separate kinds of reality, and he came up with a formula to show how they were related.

A new paradigm in any field of science is essentially a declaration of war. The new paradigm always has to fight hard for acceptance because its implications are so confrontational, so vast, and so frighteningly unpredictable. People "resist its challenges with deep emotional reactions, since those challenges threaten to destroy their very perception and experience of reality, indeed their entire world" (185.1). Power blocs emerge during a paradigm war, each arguing on its own terms that the other paradigm is not merely weak but totally false and misleading (186.6).

Not wishing to declare war on all previous paradigms of Christian mission, let us note some differences between paradigm shifts in theology and paradigm wars in the sciences.

- A new theological paradigm does not necessarily cancel the old ones the way a new scientific paradigm does. Certainly no paradigm can cancel the importance of God's revelation through Israel and the Christ (187.6).

- A new theological paradigm need not insist it is absolutely right; it can admit that it is incomplete and even affected by cultural bias (186.9). Since the community defining Christian mission is now a global intercultural community, different perspectives within that community can critique each other's biases (187.8).

- A new scientific paradigm "cannot be made logically or even probabilistically compelling" for those who have not joined the group that favors it (186.7, quoting Kuhn). A new theological paradigm can, at least theoretically, make sense to outsiders.

- Scientists have to operate in one paradigm or another. In ordinary life people often straddle two theological paradigms at once (186.4).

In a word, scientific paradigms tend to be totalitarian, demanding absolute loyalty from their adherents. Theological paradigms, at least Christian ones, can afford to be much softer around the edges. "I realize that my theological approach is a 'map,' and that a map is never the actual 'territory.' ... Although I believe that my map is the best, I accept that there are other types of maps and also that, at least in theory, one of those may be better than mine since I can only know in part (cf. 1 Cor. 13:12)" (187.4). The commitment we give to any theological paradigm is therefore wholehearted and provisional, wholehearted because we hold back nothing from our Lord, provisional because our Lord makes us his witnesses, not his know-it-alls.

This is certainly no time for half-hearted commitment. "The Christian church in general and the Christian mission in particular are today confronted with issues they have never even dreamt of and which are crying out for responses that are both relevant to the times and in harmony with the essence of the Christian faith" (188.7). The world is simply not the same as it was a century or two ago. For example:

- The West (including Western theology) is no longer seen as the world's savior but the world's dominator and abuser.

- Racism, sexism, and other long-held but oppressive ideas are under attack.

- There is doubt about the meaning and the possibility of so-called "progress."

- There is a growing sense of unity as one race on one planet.

- We have the technology and the weapons to destroy the race and the planet.

- Freedom of religion is regarded as a basic human right, creating some ambiguity about the call for conversion to Christianity.

Our challenge is not to tackle these changes one at a time but to step back and look at the whole pattern, the whole paradigm that is changing (189.5). Fortunately we are not the first generation to have to attempt such a massive challenge and transition. It has happened at least four times in the last two thousand years. By examining those four paradigm changes in church history, we may get some helpful perspective on the size of our present challenge and the ways we may begin to deal with it. For a preview of the next four chapters, see the summary in Table 8 (p. 84).

Chapter 6

Good Ideas of Life and Love

The Missionary Paradigm
of the Eastern Church, AD 100–600

(Bosch, TM, pp. 190–213)

For God so loved the world that he gave his one and only Son, that whoever believes in him shall not perish but have eternal life. (John 3:16)

Several interconnected changes occurred in the theory and practice of mission during the second to sixth centuries. Perhaps the central one was the transformation of the Christian message from a breaking news story to a creed. As with all paradigm changes in mission, this one was an attempt to incarnate the faith and communicate the gospel in terms relevant to the situation. Of course, there are always pros and cons to such attempts, but before describing and evaluating the Eastern paradigm of mission, let us consider the situation it was trying to address.

THE CONTEXT OF MISSION

In the early second century, Christianity was a banned religious movement in the Roman Empire, yet it continued to spread mostly because of the winsome lives of ordinary Christians (211.7). As Christian leaders in the second and third centuries gradually tried to win a hearing with the upper classes in the empire, they reformulated the Christian faith using some of the categories of the pagan Greek philosophers (whom the elite respected) while contrasting Christian religious practice with the rituals of the pagan Near Eastern religions (which the elite despised).

Early in the fourth century, the ban on Christianity was lifted, and by the late fourth century all citizens in the Roman Empire were required by the emperor to be Christians. After the political tide turned in their favor, the Christians kept refining their concepts and doctrines. They produced creeds and (ironically) with the aim of preserving the unity of the church throughout the empire got these official positions of the church enforced against heretical groups with the emperor's power.

Their two mission challenges in these two phases of this period were therefore to win upper-class respectability for an illegal religious movement and, from the fourth century onward, to carry on mission from a position of power. They tackled both challenges by refining their ideas and attempting to prove that these were good ideas, fundamentally sound, philosophically defensible (194.7).

THE MISSIONARY MESSAGE

The message which the church tailored for this situation was a message of life and love. Who in his right mind would persecute such a positive message? Or who would object to an emperor imposing such a healthy thing? Surely if the message were understood it would be accepted and welcomed. Consider its positive aspects.

1. The key mission text for the Orthodox is a verse of life and love, John 3:16 (quoted at the beginning of this chapter; 208.8). The Orthodox bring this verse into the present much more than the Western churches do, that is, they put more emphasis on sharing in eternal life now than on avoiding "perishing" under God's judgment after we die (209.1).

2. Mission is "founded on the *love of God*" (208.8). The message is that in love, God has taken the initiative by sending Christ to seek the lost sheep. Another way to say this is that God is not the one keeping score on human beings in the game of life; he is the one who gets into the game and helps them play. "Christ did not come primarily to put away human sin, but to restore in humans the image of God and give them life" (209.3).

3. The Christian community, gathered in the church, is the one human community that is hot-wired into the life and love of God. The liturgy of the church is specifically designed to conduct God's life to his people, restoring his image in them. We might even say that the church in worship is like a time machine — God's future for the cosmos becomes present in the church through the liturgy. This is "heaven on earth," a key phrase for all Orthodox (209.5). The future is now.

4. God's life and love spill over from the Christian community in all directions. They extend to society, culture, the state, and even the world of nature. "Not only humanity, but also the whole universe 'participates in the restoration and finds its orientation again in glorifying God' " (209.7, quoting Anastasios).

What good news! How logical! And how silly of anyone either to oppose it if they have political power or to resist it if any political power imposes it on them.

THE AIM OF MISSION

The spillover of God's life and love into the world is not an accident but a deliberate intention of corporate worship and a necessary result of it. "The mission of the church into the world, the second liturgy [literally, 'service' or 'worship'], rests upon the radiating and transforming power of the Liturgy [done in the church building]. The Liturgy makes the liturgy possible" (210.7).

The church gathered becomes the kingdom of God, receiving his life and love as it receives his transforming influence. The church then spreads out during the week as individual Christians share the water of life and especially as they call non-Christians to come into the fountain of life, the church, and drink for themselves (207.1).

In other words, mission means, "calling people to become members of the Christian community in a visible concrete form" (207.3, quoting Bria). To change the image slightly, we could say the capacity of a pipe depends on its diameter. As more people join the church, its diameter increases and it can pipe more of God's life and love into the world. This is "service" to God, for it releases more of the love that is pent up in him, eager to deluge the world. The more his life and love flow out, the more things will be brought into harmony as they were meant to be and the more glory and praise will flow back to him — the ultimate aim of mission.

THE METHODS OF MISSION

1. Defend the faith or die for it

"It is to the Greeks that we owe *the intellectual discipline of theology* and the classical formulations of the Christian faith" (206.5), but theology was not an armchair pastime in the early years of Christianity. The second- and third-century church fathers were known collectively as the "apologists," that is, those involved in apologetics (defense of the faith), not those "apologizing" for it. Many who spoke up for the faith were martyred for it. In fact, the word "martyr" comes from the Greek word for a witness. By sealing their arguments with their own blood, these Christians showed what mission looks like under fire.

2. Enlarge the church

We have already noted the importance of official membership in the church as an institution. It is simply not possible in the Orthodox point of view to think of making individual converts who may or may not decide to become involved in the life of a local congregation of believers (207.1). Such people are not "converts" at all. Their Christianity is an imaginary Christianity, a mere set of ideas. Like a phantom or ghost, it floats around without embodiment in a group of people. It has no substance.

3. Treasure the liturgy

"The major manifestation of the missionary activity of the Orthodox church lies in its celebration of the liturgy. The light of mercy that shines in the liturgy should act as a center of attraction to those who still live in the darkness of paganism" (207.8, quoting Rose). The mission of the church is to be itself, especially in its worship. Since God is transforming the church into his image and human beings were created for him, they have to be drawn to him when they see the church, just as weary travelers are drawn to run for home once they get a glimpse of it in the distance.

4. Send out the monks

"When Christianity became the official religion of the Empire and persecutions ended, the monk succeeded the martyr as the expression of unqualified witness and protest against worldliness" (202.1). The monks "laid down their lives" in a different way than the martyrs, but no less completely. The story of the spread of Eastern Christianity over the centuries is mostly the story of the monks, who went out into foreign territory as the ambassadors of the bishops and bearers of God's life and love.

AN EVALUATION OF THE EASTERN PARADIGM

The good news in Eastern dress certainly has much to commend it. The biblical themes of life and love are prominent and clearly contrasted with their opposites. Using some of the tools of Greek philosophy, the church was able "to distinguish truth from fantasy, to repudiate magic, superstition, fatalism, astrology, and idolatry" (200.8). In particular, the church for the most part fended off two heresies that denied the importance of life in this world — Montanism, which announced that the end of the world was imminent, and gnosticism, which declared that the material world was evil and the only hope of humans was special "knowledge" of the secrets of the universe (199.5).

The Eastern paradigm placed a very high value on the church and tightly wove together the concepts of church, worship, and mission. The horizon for mission stretched beyond human beings to nature and indeed the whole universe. The martyrs and monks paid the ultimate price as they went about mission. The theologians achieved an intellectual success and produced a coherent system, still allowing for the huge, inexplicable mystery of the Trinity at the heart of it. Unlike the gnostics, they valued reason very highly. Unlike the Greek philosophers, they did not trust reason as their ultimate guide.

Unfortunately several of these wonderful strengths of the Eastern paradigm had a not so wonderful flip side. "The Christian message was in the process of being transformed from the announcement of God's imminent reign to the proclamation of the only true and universal religion of humankind" (196.7).

Table 4
Mission and Omissions in the Orthodox Paradigm

Emphases	What got lost?
1. Christianity as a universal religion	1. Christianity as more than a religion—good news that affects every aspect of life
2. The church is the kingdom of God and his eternal life is with us now	2. The expectation of the return of the Messiah
3. Clear doctrines	3. Clear ethical demands
4. The church and state are united	4. The state-free nature of Christian witness
5. John	5. Paul

Let us take a closer look at the topics listed in Table 4.

1. "The God of the Old Testament and primitive Christianity came to be identified with the general idea of God of Greek metaphysics; God is referred to as Supreme Being, substance, principle, unmoved mover. . . . It became more important to reflect on what God is in himself than to consider the relationship in which people stand to God. Behind all this lies the [Platonic] notion that the abstract idea is more real than the historical. Therefore, what pagans were really in need of was an adequate doctrine of God" (194.8). If events matter less than ideas, mission will be less about passing on the good news of an event than communicating right doctrines. "Preaching came to focus almost exclusively on the topic of God and the individual soul" (197.8).

2. With the healthy emphasis on the transforming presence of God's love and life during the liturgy, there came an unhealthy loss of emphasis on the sudden, future coming of the messianic kingdom. The kingdom was already available and believers would gradually grow into it. The idea of gradual improvement slid over into the idea of earning one's way up a series of stages of spiritual maturity by good deeds and prayers (198.3). The Holy Spirit was emphasized as the one who sanctifies, that is, helps the believer up this series of stages. The idea of the Holy Spirit as the driving force for mission faded away (201.2).

3. The contrast between a focus on doctrine and a focus on behavior is evident when we contrast the fourth-century Nicene Creed and the first-century Sermon on the Mount. The Sermon, in both its content and its structure,

focuses on the conduct of the follower of Jesus and says virtually nothing in philosophical language. The creed is just the opposite (195.3).

4. At the time Emperor Constantine made Christianity legal, the church was like an infant that has never before seen a cobra. The child does not know how to charm the snake. It does not even know not to pick it up by the sharp end. When the church announced a political theology in which the church and state were inseparably united, it did not know what poison it was letting into its system. It could not foresee what historians have noted since: "Orthodox churches tended to become ingrown, excessively nationalistic, and without a concern for those outside" (212.9). The bite of the pro-Christian state proved more deadly to mission than the bite of the anti-Christian state had ever been.

5. Indicative of the preceding four shifts was the fact that the Orthodox relied on the writings of John almost to the exclusion of the writings of Paul. Life and love are John's themes. Eschatology (including the "grace period") is Paul's. "There is probably no area in which the Hellenistic church differed so profoundly from primitive Jewish Christianity as that of its eschatology and understanding of history" (196.1).

"It should not bother us that, during the epoch under discussion, the Christian faith was perceived and experienced in new and different ways. The Christian faith is intrinsically incarnational; therefore, unless the church chooses to remain a foreign entity, it will always enter into the context in which it happens to find itself" (190.9). From a distance we may critique each paradigm, but we ought not to dismiss any of them. Rather let us continue to see them in relation to their situations so that we may better see ourselves in relation to our own.

YOUR VIEWS AND YOUR CONTEXT

24. What is the highest compliment you can pay to the Eastern Orthodox paradigm of mission as described in this chapter?

25. What is the most serious criticism you can make of it?

26. If you are Orthodox or have some previous knowledge of Orthodoxy, how accurate do you believe Bosch's description is? Where would you refine it?

Note: other questions on the Orthodox paradigm are included at the end of the next chapter (see questions 30–32 on pp. 60–61). They involve a comparison of Orthodox and Catholic perspectives.

Chapter 7

Filling the Master's House

The Missionary Paradigm of the Roman Catholic Church, AD 600–1500

(Bosch, TM, pp. 214–38)

Then the master told his servant, "Go out to the roads and country lanes and make them come in, so that my house will be full." (Luke 14:23)

Throughout the period covered in this chapter, the Western part of the Church (today the Roman Catholic Church) agreed with the Eastern part of the church (the Orthodox) on two central points that the New Testament writers had not imagined. First, the powers of church and state belonged together and, second, the gospel was more like a creed than a breaking news story. But there was increasing East-West polarization about what the creed really meant concerning salvation and how that salvation was to be promoted. The polarization started with Augustine of Hippo, in what is now Algeria.

To have any chance of understanding the complexities of the overlapping models of mission[1] during this nine-hundred-year period (as well as the substantial parts of this chapter that come before or after that era), we need a basic timeline as a reference point (Figure 3, p. 56). In this timeline, a vertical bar indicates the date of an event, an ordinary X indicates the life span of an individual, and a wide X indicates a trend longer than a lifetime.

---

1. The models are so complex that Bosch entirely leaves out the part of the story dealing with Roman Catholic mission in places Western powers did not colonize — China, Japan, and India. He may have done so because the innovative mission approach of the Jesuits there mostly occurred after 1500 and was rejected by the papacy from the late eighteenth century until Vatican II. See reference to William Burrows's article on "radical inculturation" as a "seventh missionary paradigm" (below p. 141).

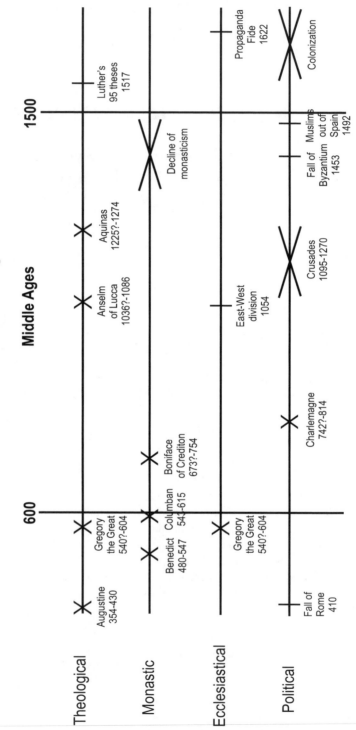

Figure 3
Timeline: Mission in the Middle Ages

AUGUSTINE'S RESPONSE TO THE FALL OF ROME

By all accounts Augustine is a landmark thinker in Christian history.[2] His own radical conversion from an immoral life to Christian faith as a young man colored his thinking a great deal in later life at a time when the church faced massive theological and political crises. In the face of these challenges, Augustine passionately taught that salvation was a gift to anyone and everyone who belonged to the church. Good human actions could not earn it (as Pelagius implied), nor could bad human actions forfeit it (as the Donatists believed) (217.9).

While Augustine, as a bishop, was dueling with Pelagians and Donatists in Carthage (part of Tunisia today), Rome fell to the "barbarians," that is, the non-Christian Goths. This shook the foundations of the worldview of most Christians, who assumed that the church and the empire were divinely interlocked and unconquerable (220.3).

Augustine attempted to encourage the shaken Christians by persuading them to look at the world differently. He divided reality into two levels, a spiritual level and an earthly level, with the spiritual level being superior. He then asserted the authority of the church on the spiritual level, where it (supposedly) could not be challenged by any earthly power (221.4). In other words, Rome had fallen but the "city of God" had not, and it never could.

Augustine's "city of God" (also the title of his multivolume work written over fourteen years) is not a city as such but a "spiritual society" including all those who live under God's reign as they travel toward their heavenly home. The contrasting "city of this world" is not entirely evil but, like all things human, it is too evil ever to achieve the peace and justice for which it strives. It will need guidance and help from God.

AIM AND METHODS OF MISSION

The mission of the "city of God" is to bring its own citizens into God's eternal salvation and to provide in God's name the guidance needed by the "city of this world." The guidance is given partly by the church advising the state and partly by citizens of the "city of God" living in light of their heavenly destination. Let us look at three models of mission, each based on a different part of this definition of mission.

---

2. Many Roman Catholics do not agree with Bosch's choice of Augustine (fifth century) rather than Aquinas (thirteenth century) as the thinker who defined the paradigm of medieval Catholicism. Bosch's choice leads him to spend a lot of time in this chapter discussing the relationship of political control and mission, leaving the impression that medieval Catholic mission theology was primarily a political theology. Had he balanced the picture by including Aquinas (whom he only mentions four times in passing in the chapter), he would have placed more emphasis on the planting and formation of the church by apolitical methods and structures. My chapter summarizes Bosch's view without attempting to rewrite it to give Aquinas the attention he deserves. For a thorough description of Aquinas's significance for theology of mission, see Stephen Bevans and Roger Schroeder, *Constants in Context* (Maryknoll, N.Y.: Orbis Books, 2004), 164–67.

Mission via political control within Christendom (220.1)

Baptism confers citizenship in the "city of God." The governments of Christian territories should protect all their citizens from anything that might take them off the path to eternal salvation. They should even protect them from themselves. If any citizens stray from church teachings, Christian rulers are to discipline them with fines, imprisonment, torture, or even execution. All this pressure, which looks "totally incomprehensible and indefensible" to us today (230.6), was regarded as discipline intended for the eternal good of the citizen concerned.

Mission via war and colonization (222.6)

As power gradually exercised its corrupting influence on the church, it became acceptable for violence to be used against those outside the church as well (also "for their own good," of course). At first this was only via "indirect missionary wars," Christian rulers subduing pagan peoples in order to open the door for missionary proclamation to them (223.5). In situations like Charlemagne's conquest of the Saxons, this turned into "direct missionary wars" (224.5) in which the terms of surrender included baptism.

Eventually violence became so palatable that mission was excluded. Some regarded it as praiseworthy before God to rid the earth of unbelievers rather than convert them (225.4). This theology of war grew during the European Crusades into Palestine, which were not "missionary wars" since they were never intended nor expected to convert the conquered Muslims. They were only wars to keep Christendom itself, including its ancient sites, free from Muslim control (225.1).

The pendulum swung back toward the "indirect missionary war" in the late fifteenth century when Spain and Portugal embarked on global colonization. As in the Crusades, their initial aim in the Americas, Africa, and Asia was to establish political control over non-Christian peoples. Unlike the Crusaders, however, they believed that the peoples they conquered could be converted (though they did not force conversion and baptism on them). They only made the areas safe for missionaries.

Mission via model citizens of the "city of God" (monasticism; 230.2)

At the same time that some were exploring the above forms of "mission by force," a completely different approach to mission was emerging that depended on modeling and persuasion, not on power. This was the monastic movement, initially composed of two main strains, the Celtic and the Benedictine. "From the fifth century to the twelfth, the monastery was not only the center of culture and civilization, but also of mission.... In the midst of a world ruled by the love of self, the monastic communities were a visible sign and preliminary realization of a world ruled by the love of God" (230.8). They were the places on earth where the "city of God" could best be (fore)seen.

Monks are popularly seen today as people who detach themselves from the world but in the Middle Ages there was a very close connection between monks and mission. It is true that they did seek to live pure lives detached from worldly ambitions and influences, but it is also true that "the citizens of the heavenly city were actively seeking the peace and good order of the earthly city" (232.6).

"The monks were poor, and they worked incredibly hard; they plowed, hedged, drained morasses, cleared away forests, did carpentry, thatched, and built roads and bridges. . . . They lifted the hearts of the poor and neglected peasants and inspired them" (232.2). Through waves of destructive invasion by northern barbarians during the Middle Ages, the monks demonstrated the resilience that gave hope to the whole of European society, "for theirs was a 'spirituality of the long haul' and not of instant success" (232.9).

The monks did not even seem to know words like "force," "punish," "strategy," and "leverage." In fact, many did not even do what they did in order to persuade anyone of anything. They were simply serving God and renouncing the down side of the world. For example, even a pilgrimage might be viewed not as a missionary journey but as a form of renunciation of the comforts of home. "Mission" happened naturally, almost incidentally, along the way, as the monks helped other travelers. Yet for centuries the monks had massive influence on European society religiously, economically, and socially. They transformed a continent while attracting so little attention to themselves that history books seldom mention them.

The missionary message

The fall of Rome meant a loss of governing authority for Christians. The medieval paradigm of mission (with the exception of the Celtic monks) is very largely an attempt to reassert the governing authority of the church at the spiritual level and to build the missionary activity of the church on that reestablished authority.

The key mission text in this paradigm is an authority text, "Make them come in," or "Compel them to come in" (Luke 14:23). In the parable from which this verse is taken, the master sends his servants out on a mission, gathering people for his banquet and doing whatever it takes to fill the banquet hall. When an entire philosophy of mission is grounded on this verse, the whole thing turns on whether "whatever it takes" includes the use of force. The papacy said yes. The monks said no.

AN EVALUATION OF THE ROMAN CATHOLIC PARADIGM

In our day it is easy to criticize the medieval Roman Catholic paradigm and rather hard to find anything good to say about it, especially since the Roman

Catholic Church itself has rejected most of it since the Second Vatican Council (1962–65). "Still, our appraisal cannot only be a negative one. Was anything wrong with the idea of attempting to create a Christian civilization, to shape laws consonant with biblical teaching, to place kings and emperors under the explicit obligation of Christian discipleship?" (237.6).

Perhaps the key issue is whether "creating a Christian civilization" means imposing one (as the church often tried to do via an alliance with the state) or demonstrating one (as the monks did). The imposition of Christianity makes sense to one who believes in the view of salvation of Augustine and Anselm: "Not the reconciliation of the universe but the redemption of the soul stands in the center. This redemption is understood to be both other-worldly and individualistic.... The hope of the kingdom of God was transformed into a hope of 'heaven,' the place or state of life in which those who have done good will be rewarded" (216.8). If we then have to inflict pain on the temporary body in order to secure the welfare of the eternal soul, why not do it?

The monks, though in practice renouncing the world, did not divide this world from the next in the theoretical way that Augustine did. For the monks, the physical, everyday world was not a second-class reality but a first-class opportunity to serve God and demonstrate life under his reign. Augustine argued that the legitimacy and authority of the church did not depend on the quality of Christian life demonstrated by its members. The monks were less concerned with legitimacy and authority than with simply and humbly pleasing God by demonstrating obedience to him.[3]

YOUR VIEWS AND YOUR CONTEXT

27. What is the highest compliment you can pay to the Roman Catholic paradigm of mission as described in this chapter?

28. What is the most serious criticism you can make of it?

29. If you are Catholic or have some previous knowledge of Catholicism, how accurate do you believe Bosch's description of the medieval paradigm of mission is? Where would you refine it?

30. Creeds and formal theology were developed in the third and fourth centuries in an imperial culture dominated by Greek thought. Today some regard these developments as a great step forward in the life of the church. Others see them as a great diversion from the mission of the church as described in the New Testament. What is your view?

31. In the Orthodox and Catholic paradigms, monks played a key role in mission for more than a thousand years. Why was this so? In the new era of

---

3. I admit that this is too simplistic a contrast between Augustine and the monks, but in this short chapter it will have to suffice. Many more nuances await the reader in Bosch's own chapter on which the above is based.

mission before us today, how relevant might a revived or new monastic movement be?

32. In the Orthodox and Catholic paradigms, partnership between the church and the state is seen as an important aid to mission. How did this partnership fit into each paradigm and make sense as part of the whole?

Chapter 8

Justification by Faith

The Missionary Paradigm
of the Protestant Reformation,
AD 1500–1800

(Bosch, TM, pp. 239–61)

> *I am not ashamed of the gospel, because it is the power of God for the salvation of everyone who believes: first for the Jew, then for the Gentile. For in the gospel a righteousness from God is revealed, a righteousness that is by faith from first to last, just as it is written: "The righteous will live by faith."* (Rom. 1:16–17)

So little was said about mission by Luther and Calvin and so little mission was undertaken by their churches during the Reformation that it has been doubted whether they had any paradigm of mission at all. The Roman Catholics considered the lack of Protestant outreach to pagans and Jews as clear evidence that the Reformers were heretics (243.9). During the sixteenth-century Protestant scramble for each church to define itself as the "true" church (248.5), all the definitions of the church revolved around "what happens inside its four walls, not in terms of its calling in the world" (249.2). It seems not to have occurred to anyone that the true church might be the one most passionately driven to mission by the Spirit of God.

On the other hand, some recent scholars have argued that these criticisms "misunderstand the basic [missionary] thrust of their [the Reformers'] theology and ministry" (244.6). To understand these conflicting views of the Reformation and mission, let us examine the roots and the core theology of the Reformation. We will consider its ambivalence about mission and note how variations of the Protestant paradigm of mission developed on the Anabaptist margin of the Reformation as well as in the Lutheran Pietist movement and Calvinist Puritan movement a century later.

DESPERATE PESSIMISM
AND AMAZING GRACE

"Augustine had rediscovered Paul for the fifth century; Luther rediscovered him for the sixteenth" (240.1). A key part of Luther's multilayered rediscovery was the bias toward pessimism about the human condition in contrast to the prevailing optimism about human potential to develop ourselves into God's likeness and win his favor by good works.

Augustine, opposing Pelagius's optimism and thinking he was following Paul, had been quite pessimistic about humanity; hence his strong emphasis on grace as the only hope for sinful humanity. However, by the peak of the Middle Ages, the pendulum had swung back toward optimism about humanity, especially human reason. This view was best expressed in the "magnificent synthesis" theology of Thomas Aquinas. Working along Aristotelian lines, he assigned everything on earth and in heaven a logical (almost scientific) place (239.9). Aquinas "solved" everything and brought it all within reach of human reason. Humans still needed grace but not as desperately as Augustine had thought.

Luther took theology back into the world of desperation. This, however, was not the world of hopelessness. It was the door to an earth-shaking discovery of new hope, our only hope. As he reread Paul, Luther realized that "God's righteousness did not mean God's righteous punishment and wrath, but his gift of grace and mercy, which the individual may appropriate in faith" (240.4). That is, God's "righteousness" is God "setting humans right" by his gracious intervention, not crushing them for falling short of his righteous standards. God is the justifier, that is, a missionary, pro-active in love and grace, not the judge who simply waits till the end of history and then reacts to what others have done within his perfect system.

REFORMATION THEOLOGY —
A SHAKY FOUNDATION FOR MISSION

If Luther had a missionary God, did he have a missionary theology? Not exactly. We have to deal with the many basic ambiguities of Reformation theology that could (and did) work for or against mission, depending how they were interpreted (see Table 5, p. 64).

The pro-mission aspects of Reformation theology were explicitly drawn out by Nicolai among the Lutherans a generation after Luther and by Voetius among the Calvinists a century after Calvin. Philip Nicolai's *Commentary on the Kingdom of Christ* (1597) contained many promising leads toward a missionary Lutheran theology, but unfortunately these were nearly all swept away by the Lutheran theologians who followed him in the seventeenth century. Table 6 (p. 65) contrasts the promise with the actual course of events.

Table 5
Reformation Theology — For or Against Mission?

Theme	Pro-mission aspect	Anti-mission aspect
1. Justification by faith (241.3)	This discovery of the gospel is too good to keep to ourselves (242.6).	It is all up to God to decide who will be saved and how they will hear the gospel.
2. Sinfulness of humans (241.6)	Mission is God's mission; we must depend on him as we engage in it (242.8).	Nothing we do will change reality.
3. Personal experience of salvation by grace (241.8)	The salvation of each individual is valuable in God's sight (242.9).	Religion turns selfish; the life of the church as a community is neglected.
4. Priesthood of all believers (242.2)	Every Christian (lay or clergy) is called to serve God in the world (243.1).	The church disintegrates into denominations; our witness is compromised.
5. Centrality of Scriptures (242.5)	Preaching the word is central to the life and mission of the church (243.4).	The Bible almost replaces God as the basis for mission.

Voetius, who proved more influential among the Calvinists than Nicolai had been among the Lutherans, is widely recognized as "the first Protestant theologian to have developed a comprehensive 'theology of mission'" (256.9). His three stair-step aims of mission became the classic point of reference for Calvinist mission theology: (1) the conversion of the nations, (2) the planting of the church, (3) the glory of divine grace made visible (256.9). He explicitly built on the Reformation discovery of a missionary God, the fountain from which mission flows, and he defined mission broadly enough to include the whole field of activity that in the twentieth century became known as ecumenism (257.2).

Table 6
The Demise of Mission in Lutheran Theology

Theme	Nicolai's view	"Later orthodoxy" view
Great Commission (249.7)	"Fulfilled" but needs follow-through today	"Fulfilled" and thus with no application today
God's love (250.6)	Drives us to love others around us wherever God puts us	Distributed by God himself wherever he wants to
Christ's return (251.1)	A motive for mission	A motive for hunkering down and protecting our own faith as things get worse
Colonies (251.3)	Church should do mission if and when the state establishes colonies	Mission in the colonies is the responsibility of the state, not the church.

THREE MARGINAL MOVEMENTS

The fact that very few readers today — even those with some knowledge of Reformation history — have ever heard of Nicolai or Voetius should tell us something. The anti-mission aspects of Reformation theology were often the majority view. Fed up with the anti-mission mainstream and doubtful that the majority would ever see the dawning mission light, three movements on the margins of the Reformation did the most significant mission thinking and work in the sixteenth, seventeenth, and eighteenth centuries respectively — the Anabaptists, the Puritans, and the Pietists.

The Anabaptists, contemporaries of Luther and Calvin, created their own cells, congregations, and networks completely separate from the Lutheran and Calvinist churches. The two later movements developed as a "church within a church," the Pietists in the Lutheran Church and the Puritans in the Reformed Church.

The Anabaptists (sixteenth century; 245.9)

The Anabaptists, who emerged in the heyday of Luther and Calvin, broke all the rules. For a start, they radicalized the Reformation idea of the priesthood of all believers to the extent that they denied the validity of the priesthood in any of the other churches, Catholic or Protestant. They denied that baptism in those churches could make anyone a Christian, because the infants being baptized could not exercise personal faith.

This meant that Europe's church members were not Christians and "Europe was once again a mission field" (247.6). The true gospel had to be proclaimed by every true believer in obedience to the Great Commission (246.4). In their zeal they disregarded all parish boundaries and all church offices that had geographical limits. They also claimed that "church and state could under no circumstances whatsoever cooperate in mission" (246.6).

The Puritans (seventeenth century; 255.9)

While Voetius was writing his mission theology within the "Second Reformation" movement in Holland, the parallel "Puritan" movement developed in the Calvinist churches of England and Scotland. Puritan mission theology wove seven themes together — predestination, the glory of God, the grace and love of God, colonies as theocracies, an optimistic theology of history, the superiority of Western culture, and very little explicit emphasis on the Great Commission. Let us take a closer look at some of these.

Predestination may seem to undercut all mission, and sometimes it has. Why bother trying to persuade people to accept the gospel if God has already decided who will be saved? In the Calvinist view, predestination applies both to this life and the next. Some are predestined for mission so that others can hear the gospel they are predestined to receive. If understood in this way, predestination can be a powerful incentive for mission.

The ideal of theocracy (an absolute mistake from an Anabaptist point of view) was central to the Puritans. Mission meant not so much the evangelization and conversion of individuals as the creation and nurture of Christian colonies, establishing "in the 'wilderness' a socio-political system in which God himself would be the real ruler" (259.4).

The Puritan gospel was not a set of timeless truths but a message for a particular moment in God's sovereign plan for history. Calvin had believed in three epochs in the history of the church — the apostolic era, the era dominated by the anti-Christ (the papacy, from his point of view), and the era of the great expansion of the church. He believed he lived in the second era. The Puritans, a century later, accepted his outline and believed that in their day the third era was dawning.

They therefore embarked for the New England colonies eagerly and confidently anticipating what the Almighty God would do there in the new era. They did not know exactly what to expect, but they were pretty sure that culturally it would look more like England than the indigenous cultures.

The Pietists (eighteenth century; 252.6)

The Anabaptists under widespread, severe persecution had waned as a missionary force by the late sixteenth century, but several of their emphases were taken up in the early eighteenth century by the Pietists. "Concepts such as repentance, conversion, the new birth, and sanctification received new meaning. A disciplined life rather than sound doctrine, subjective experience of the individual rather than ecclesiastical authority, practice rather than theory — these were the hallmarks of the new movement" (252.9). Unlike the Anabaptists, the Pietists did not attack the basic theology of the mainstream church. They simply took it for granted and went on to what really mattered in their opinion, personal piety and its corollary, mission.

The Pietists did, however, make a frontal attack on the mainstream Lutheran view of mission, which by their day was abysmal. Bartholomäus Ziegenbalg blasted the theologians "because of their view that the church had already been planted everywhere; that the office of apostle had vanished; that God's grace no longer worked as powerfully as it did in the beginning; that those who were still pagans were under a curse; that God, if he wished to convert them, would do so without human effort" (253.1).

The Pietists gave up on the mission potential of the Lutheran Church (their church) as a whole. Inside a church that was going nowhere, the Pietists established a small revived community to be the bearer of mission (253.8). They did not wait to be sent by political authorities into the colonies but simply went when and where Christ was sending them. They did not separate spiritual and physical aspects of their service to the world. In ways reminiscent of Catholic monasticism, "Ordinary men and women, most of them simple artisans, went literally to the ends of the earth, devoted themselves for life to people often living in the most degrading circumstances, identified with them, and lived the gospel in their midst" (255.7).

These movements, especially the Pietists, provided the root from which the global mission movement of Protestantism would shoot forth in the nineteenth century. We also need to mention one "movement" that never took off but literally died with its champion, nobleman Justinian von Welz, a generation before the Pietists. His idea was that "hermit-missionaries" should be sent out all over the world by a "Jesus-Loving Society." They should be "people marked by holiness and personal piety." Ostracized by the Lutheran theological establishment, he himself went to Surinam in 1666, "where he died, probably in that same year, 'a sacrifice to orthodox intransigence'" (252.5, quoting Scherer).

The Reformation theological paradigm could be a stepping-stone to mission or, as the sad reaction to von Welz shows, a stumbling-stone preventing it. Luther and Calvin were dead set on getting the church's doctrine right, assuming that the influence of right ideas expressed in right words would percolate through the church and transform it into everything God wanted it to be. One wonders what their theologies would have looked like if they had made mission rather than justification their doctrinal center.

YOUR VIEWS AND YOUR CONTEXT

33. Agree or disagree and explain your reasons: *Martin Luther believed in a missionary God; Thomas Aquinas did not. This was the core theological difference between medieval Catholicism and the Protestant Reformation.*

34. Once a theology puts major emphasis on personal experience of salvation by grace, how will its definition of the purpose and methods of mission change? How will they differ from those of a theology where the establishment of the institutional church in a new region is the primary goal?

35. In Table 5 (p. 64), Reformation Theology, rank the five themes in the left column according to their potential for motivating your church to mission today. Start with the one with the most potential. Briefly explain your ranking. (If none of the five are strong motivators, write two theological themes that are.)

36. Voetius said the three-step goal of mission is: (1) the conversion of the nations, (2) the planting of the church, (3) the glory of divine grace made visible. How adequate is this view as a framework for a theology of mission in your country or region today?

37. Which of the marginal movements contributed most to what you consider a sound theology of mission today — the Anabaptists, the Puritans, the Pietists? What did that one group contribute and why do you consider it so significant?

Chapter 9

Enlightened Mission?

The Fragmented Missionary Paradigm(s) of Protestantism, AD 1800–2000

(Bosch, TM, pp. 262–345)

Then Jesus came to them and said, "All authority in heaven and on earth has been given to me. Therefore go and make disciples of all nations, baptizing them in the name of the Father and of the Son and of the Holy Spirit, and teaching them to obey everything I have commanded you. And surely I am with you always, to the very end of the age." (Matt. 28:18–20)

In *Transforming Mission,* the chapter on mission after the Enlightenment is longer than the chapters on the Orthodox, Catholic, and Reformation mission paradigms combined. This is appropriate since our most important missiological task today is to recognize the Enlightenment assumptions in our mission theory and practice. We must move beyond those assumptions if our mission is to be relevant to the postmodern era, which is largely rejecting them.[1]

SHIFTING WORLDVIEWS

A worldview is a pattern that includes, among other things, a view of God (or gods), human power structures, human beings, and nature. As a whole, the pattern tells people where they fit and what they are worth. The Enlightenment worldview can be understood if we look at its evolution, starting with the medieval worldview, which for some centuries after Aquinas appeared to be the last word in worldviews. How could anyone improve on the "perfect system"? But the

---

1. This approach to church history, giving the most attention to the most recent part of it because that has shaped us most, is one that Bosch believed strongly in. He once remarked to me that if he were going to teach church history again in South Africa, he would teach it backward, starting with the prominent churches there and tracing them back to their convergence in the New Testament.

Table 7
The Validation of Human Beings in Four Worldviews

Medieval	Renaissance & Reformation	Enlightenment	
		Age of Revolution	Age of Science
God ⇨ Church ⇨ Kings & nobles ⇨ Humans in general ⇨ Nature	God ⟹ ~~Church~~ ⇨ Kings & nobles ⇨ Humans in general ⇨ Nature	God ⟹ ~~Church~~ ~~Kings & nobles~~ Humans in general ⇨ Nature	~~God~~ ~~Church~~ ~~Kings & nobles~~ Humans in general ⇦ Nature

perfect system gradually unraveled from the sixteenth century through the nineteenth as outlined in Table 7. The "Enlightenment" includes the two columns on the right, which overlapped in time.

The arrows indicate how each entity received its philosophical validation, its right to a place in the grand scheme of things. For example, in the medieval worldview, God was self-validating, the church was validated by God, kings by the church, humans in general by the kings, and nature by humans.

In the Reformation, the church as an institution broke up and subsequently no church could claim global influence over kings as the papacy had during the Middle Ages. In the Age of Revolution (late eighteenth century), the French and American revolutions challenged the "divine right of kings," which on our chart is represented by the arrow from God to kings in the "Renaissance and Reformation" column. In the revolutionary worldview, that arrow goes straight from God to ordinary citizens.

In the Age of Science (seventeenth and eighteenth centuries), God was gradually eliminated from the picture (though key founders of the Enlightenment such as Bacon and Descartes did not make this part of the worldview shift themselves). With God sidelined or completely ruled out, nature was seen as self-validating simply because it was there. Humans were validated because they were a part of nature. Humans, if it seems reasonable to them, may create governments, churches, and perhaps even gods, but none of these supposed authorities are part of "nature" and none are validated directly by nature. None can therefore ever have any good reason to go against the "human rights" that all human individuals enjoy because they are born as part of nature.

FIVE THREADS OF THE ENLIGHTENMENT WORLDVIEW

It may be helpful to isolate several threads running through the Enlightenment worldview introduced above. These threads will be more or less visible at many places in our later discussion of the mission paradigm of the modern era.[2]

Thread 1. *Human reason* was regarded as nature's gift to each human being. Since nature was defined as the world that can be observed with the five senses, reason was limited to processing the data that come through those five channels. Data coming from other channels such as tradition or religion was to be doubted, not trusted.

Thread 2. Humans realized that though they were a part of nature, they were also (by the human faculty of reason) able to *detach themselves theoretically*

---

2. Bosch outlines seven threads, which I have simplified to five. My threads 1, 2, 3 and 5 equal his 1, 2, 3 and 5. My thread 4 combines his threads 4, 6, and 7. He works through his list three separate times: first to describe the components (264.1–267.9), second to describe the impact of each component on Christian faith (267.9–273.6), and third to suggest ways we should move beyond each of the components in a new paradigm of mission (352.1–362.8).

from nature while they studied it, or even while they studied other human beings. "Nature ceased to be 'creation' and was no longer people's teacher, but the object of their analysis" (264.5).

Thread 3. As they analyzed nature, they assumed that nature itself operated entirely by *cause and effect,* "a simple, mechanistic, billiard-ball-type causality. ... All that is needed [to transform the world] is complete knowledge of these laws of cause and effect. The human mind becomes the master" (265.4). Anything, absolutely anything, would be possible once enough humans spent enough time studying it, gathering all the relevant facts (266.8).

Thread 4. In this whole process, they had no doubt that nature was really there and that humans could accurately see and experience it. Unlike political or religious institutions, which come into being only after humans, nature was there before humans existed. Knowledge of nature was *"factual, value-free, and neutral"* — birds really do fly whether we see them or not, whether we believe it or not, whether we like it or not (266.5). If we want to know whether they fly, we just watch. This is the only reasonable way to look at the real world.

Thread 5. "A central creed of the Enlightenment was ... *faith in humankind.* Its progress was assured by the free competition of individuals pursuing their happiness" (267.4, my italics). Since all humans had received from nature the gift of Reason, it followed that all humans were naturally reasonable people. They could be expected to do reasonably well in life, especially if they were freed from the traditions and religious ideas that were based on history and conformity rather than reason. Enlightenment people "were convinced that they had both the ability and the will to remake the world in their own image" (265.7).

IMPLICATIONS OF THE FIVE THREADS
FOR CHRISTIANITY

Undermining the appeal of Christianity to "Enlightened" non-Christians

The first three threads (natural human reason, detachment from nature, and cause-effect explanations of reality) took away the reasons for Christian faith, at least the reasons that had been emphasized in the medieval era.

Thread 1. In the Middle Ages and the Reformation, Christianity had been artic- ulated as an answer to the problem of human sinfulness. In the Enlightenment, *people were regarded as essentially good* and reasonable by nature. Christianity was an answer to a problem they did not have. God was a human illusion, perhaps useful in a pre-Enlightened era but now quite beside the point or even a harmful "opiate" (269.5, referring to Marx).

Thread 2. In the Middle Ages and the Reformation, nature and society were always defined in relationship to God. The Enlightenment led to the development first of the "natural sciences" and later of the "social sciences." In both types of science, the key was *careful observation* by a human being, not the connection between the observed thing and God. God was not needed to help human beings observe things.

Thread 3. The *cause-effect explanations* of all reality affected non-Christian perceptions of the Christian message in two ways. The more obvious was that miracles were ruled out since they violate the inviolable rule that every observable effect in nature must have an observable natural cause (273.1). The subtler but perhaps more serious influence was that the Christian message itself was disregarded because it dealt with the question of the purpose of human life. The Enlightenment had decided not to ask this question since it could never be answered by a cause-effect investigation (271.3). Questions about purpose were a waste of time.

In sum, from an Enlightenment perspective, "The Christian faith is severely questioned, contemptuously repudiated, or studiously ignored" (268.5).

Affecting the way Christians saw their faith and their mission

Like all worldview shifts, the Enlightenment greatly affected not only the non-Christians who welcomed it but also (though unconsciously) the Christians trying to oppose it. The fourth and fifth threads are most relevant here.

Thread 4. The Enlightenment made a hard and fast distinction between *"facts,"* which had to do with reality, and *"values,"* which had to do with opinions. Christians generally bought this fact-value distinction, but two groups of Christians dealt with it in quite different ways (272.4). One group said that the Bible belonged to the world of "facts," and that the stories of the Bible were an objective reality just like nature as a whole. The idea of "biblical inerrancy" was developed among this group in the nineteenth century. The other group said the Bible belonged to the world of "values," and (in a way resembling the two-tiered worldview of Aquinas) the world of values was superior to the world of facts.

Thread 5. The Enlightenment idea of *progress* had a huge impact on mission thinking in the nineteenth and twentieth centuries. "Sometimes it manifested itself as the belief that the entire world would soon be converted to the Christian faith; at other times Christianity was regarded as an irresistible power in the process of reforming the world, eradicating poverty, and restoring justice for all" (271.5). Another effect came from the Enlightenment faith that progress would come by *individuals freely doing what seemed reasonable to them.* This "rampant individualism" (273.5) made the church peripheral to Christian life. Any person could hear from God directly, not via the church, so anyone could join the church of his or her choice, change churches at will, or even found a new church or a new mission organization.

The various Enlightenment influences on non-Christians and Christians had a paradoxical effect on Christianity globally in the past two centuries. Christianity has been undermined and marginalized by the Enlightenment in the formerly Christian countries, but at the same time, Christians motivated in part by the Enlightenment idea of progress have taken the Christian message to every corner of the globe. It has spread like wildfire in many parts of the Two-Thirds World, particularly Africa, where the Enlightenment worldview never became the dominant view.

NINE MOTIVES[3] FOR MISSION IN
THE ENLIGHTENMENT ERA

Since Protestant mission activity grew explosively from the late eighteenth through the twentieth centuries, it is hazardous to outline any one mission paradigm as typical of the whole period. However, we can look at nine motives that to varying degrees lay behind most of the mission thinking and activity of this era. We will give special attention to the ways these nine were influenced by the Enlightenment and the ways they differed from previous mission thinking (284.8). The first four are theological motives, the next three are Western imperialistic, and the last two are anthropological.[4]

Theological Motives

1. The Glory of God (285.7)

The glory of God had been a dominant motive for mission in the medieval era. The world needed to be brought under the control of the sovereign God so that his influence would set everything right and he himself would be appreciated and honored. In the seventeenth century this view came under two attacks, one from the Enlightenment and another from the orthodoxy movement among Protestant theologians.

The Enlightenment attack was one that, as we have seen, gradually replaced the idea of the sovereignty of God with the idea of cause-effect explanations. According to this view, the only reason Christians thought God was sovereign was that they did not understand nature. If they would study nature more, they would give up talking about God's "control" of everything. Mission would disappear.

---

3. Bosch speaks of "motifs" rather than "motives," but he acknowledges that the two overlap. See his note 3 in chapter 9 (529.7).

4. The sequence of the nine motives is different here than in Bosch (284–345) in order to group them topically as "theological, Western imperialistic, and anthropological." His sixth point (the millennium), becomes my third point, his ninth point (the Great Commission) becomes my fourth point. The rest of the numbers are adjusted as required by these two changes.

The attack from Protestant orthodoxy came from just the opposite perspective. Instead of God's sovereign control being disregarded or denied, it was affirmed as central and then taken to an extreme, anti-mission conclusion — the sovereign God would take care of mission on his own. Christians were bystanders.

Though the glory of God never faded away completely as a motive for mission, other motives that fit better with Enlightenment thinking were emphasized more. For example, the Enlightenment put humans into the center of the worldview; human needs became the measure of everything else, and mission was described as the meeting of human needs, whether religious or social (286.1).

2. Jesus' love (286.4)

"There was, among the Christians touched by the [Great] Awakening, a tremendous sense of gratitude for what they had received and an urgent desire to share with others, both at home and abroad, the blessings so freely shed upon them" (286.7). This gratitude was rooted in each individual's religious experience, which was a much more significant part of life in the atmosphere of the Enlightenment. In medieval Christendom all were baptized at birth. The religious experience of each person was rather incidental to life in a Christian state. There was little sense of individual gratitude to God, certainly nothing strong enough to motivate anyone to mission.

In the Pietist movement and the later Awakenings, people took Jesus' love personally. They began making incredible sacrifices for the religious and material welfare of people in other countries, people they regarded as their brothers and sisters in God's world (286.8). "There can, I believe, be no doubt that a primary motive of most missionaries was a genuine feeling of concern for others; they knew that the love of God had been shed abroad in their hearts and they were willing to sacrifice themselves for the sake of him who had died for them" (287.7).

Unfortunately this sincere and costly love was gradually polluted by a strange corollary of the Enlightenment's romantic view that indigenous peoples were "noble savages" (Rousseau; 288.9). Indigenous people were viewed as "noble" because they were innocent, and innocent because they were naïve, "unspoiled by civilization." They were therefore regarded favorably but condescendingly. They were helpless, needy, "poor heathen." "Compassion and solidarity had been replaced by pity and condescension" (290.1).

A mission text that reinforced this view was Acts 16:9, where the man in Paul's vision says, "Come over to Macedonia and help us" (289.6). In other words, the needy, heathen world is regarded positively in one important sense. It is ready and willing to receive the Christian gospel. The only missing link is the missionaries themselves.

3. The millennium (313.2)

Millennialism is "the biblical vision of a final golden age within history" (313.3, quoting Moorhead). Particularly in America this vision was hotly debated in the nineteenth century with massive implications for mission. The debate is essentially about how mission today relates to the return of Christ and how the return of Christ relates to the "millennium," the thousand-year golden age referred to in Revelation 20.

There were three parties to the debate:

- *Premillennialists* — Christ's return comes before the golden age, which can never arrive by human effort.

- *Postmillennialists* — in God's providence his chosen people will take the world into a golden age with Christ returning at its end to cap the age in glory.

- *Amillennialists* — the thousand-year golden age and the return of Jesus are both mythical concepts that should inspire us to work to establish God's kingdom on earth; it is pointless to debate which of these myths will happen first since neither will literally happen.

Let us begin with the amillennialists, since they are such obvious children of the Enlightenment. Amillennialism was most naturally at home in Unitarianism, which was the perfect Enlightenment religion. It emphasized human reason, the observable facts of human experience, and the goodness of human nature. "The Divine," for whom "God" is an overly personalized misnomer, was kept in view "only to give lift to the imagination" (324.3, quoting Hopkins).

Obviously a "Divine" of this type would not return to earth in the person of Jesus. Belief in such a return would be a red herring, misleading religion from its proper course. The golden age would arrive gradually through human effort. "The miraculous was eliminated and superseded by professionalism, efficiency, and scientific planning" (321.4). All of this assumed the Enlightenment's view that progress was natural and therefore inevitable.

Amillennialism flowered in the late nineteenth and early twentieth centuries as the American "Social Gospel" movement, which got much support in mainstream Protestantism. This activist movement argued that the philosophical advancement of the eighteenth century had led to the scientific advancement of the nine-teenth century, which would now naturally evolve into social advancement in the twentieth century to make the "kingdom of God" complete on earth.

Holding this optimistic view together was the romanticized concept of "the fatherhood of God and the brotherhood of all people" (322.1). Four radical shifts in the understanding of mission went along with this key concept:

- Other religions were not intrinsically evil (322.6).

- Evangelistic preaching was less emphasized than social involvement (322.9).

- "Salvation" referred to life in the present world rather than life after death (323.2).

- Mission was designed to affect society rather than individuals (323.5).

Over against the amillennialists, the premillennialists emerged as a loose cluster of movements — "adventism, the holiness movement, pentecostalism, fundamentalism, and conservative evangelicalism" (315.8). They affirmed virtually everything the amillennialists denied. In fact, one of the premillennialist criticisms of their opponents was that amillennialism emasculated mission as they understood it — a drive for the salvation and moral reformation of as many lost individuals as possible before the imminent return of Jesus Christ and the final judgment of humanity. Matthew 24:14 emerged as a major motivation for mission, "This gospel of the kingdom will be preached in the whole world as a testimony to all nations, and then the end will come" (316.8).

The amillennialists had welcomed the Enlightenment. The premillennialists rejected it, yet the long fingers of the Enlightenment still wrapped themselves around their minds far more than they suspected. For example, like the amillennialists, they unthinkingly held to the Enlightenment's faith in the superiority of Western culture and the importance of efficient organization for mission. Even when they tried to use the Bible against the Enlightenment, the premillennialists interpreted the Bible according to two Enlightenment ideas (316.1).

First was the right of each individual Christian to make his or her own judgment about the meaning of Scripture rather than be told by a church what the Scripture must mean. Such individual rights were unheard of in the church before the Enlightenment. Second was the concept of biblical inerrancy, which accepted the fact-value distinction of the Enlightenment and placed the Bible on the "fact" side of the line.

The inerrancy idea was an attempt to lay a philosophical foundation on which human reason could build a theology that would convince non-Christians to do the reasonable thing and accept Jesus as Lord. On an "inerrant" foundation, an inescapable theology could be built. As they tried to build this theology, evangelicals and fundamentalists were usually though unconsciously "making use of the rationalist framework of the Enlightenment paradigm" (319.7).

As the amillennialists and premillennialists drew up their battle lines, the postmillennialists were in danger of getting caught in the crossfire. Key mission leaders of the first half of the twentieth century such as John R. Mott, Robert E. Speer, and J. H. Oldham were among those postmillennialists who managed to keep lines of communication open with both of the warring factions. Like the premillennialists they believed in the importance of a life-changing personal religious experience and a literal return of Christ. Like the amillennialists they believed in the social implications of the gospel.

We will come back to this issue later as we discuss the emerging paradigm of mission, for in a sense this war is still being fought even if the battleground has shifted. The millennium itself is no longer the center of heated debate, but the relation between evangelization and liberation is, and it parallels the millennium debates of a century ago.

4. Obedience to the Great Commission (339.7)

Various mission texts were emphasized in different places at different times in this era.

- Acts 16:9 (Paul's Macedonian vision) was important in portraying the heathen world as eager for Western help.
- Matthew 24:14 (preaching before the end comes) was important to the premillennialists.
- John 10:10 (abundant life) was important to the Social Gospellers.

But the text that emerged as the guiding light for the era (except among the Social Gospel group) was the Great Commission, Matthew 28:18–20. William Carey's groundbreaking tract in 1792 had "demolished the conventional interpretation" of this verse and opened the way for its application to all Christians today (340.4). In other words, as Enlightened individuals, Christians were supposed to take the Great Commission personally.

Personal obedience to this "last command of Christ" became a dominant theme among mission promoters by the beginning of the twentieth century. It gave them powerful leverage, providing decisive motivation for many a missionary. It must be noted, however, that this emphasis on obedience "removes the church's involvement in mission from the domain of *gospel* to that of *law*" (341.7). We will need to reconsider this as we build a new paradigm of mission for the future.

Western, Imperialistic Motives

5. The gospel as part of Western culture (291.1)

The Enlightenment as the Age of Reason led into the Age of Science and "put the West at an unparalleled advantage over the rest of the world.... It was only logical that this feeling of superiority would also rub off on the 'religion of the West,' Christianity" (291.8). It was unthinkingly accepted that the best religion and the best culture would be exported as a package, "that every nation was en route to one world culture and that this culture would be essentially Western" (292.7). This Western bias ran equally through the liberal and conservative camps, with a few notable exceptions such as Rufus Anderson (297.9).

Especially toward the end of the nineteenth century, the ugly side of other cultures was painted in vivid colors in order to impress the urgency of mission on Western supporters (293.5). (This reinforced motives two and four above.) It is true that the ugly side was real and the missionary attack on it was well justified. Missionaries made huge improvements in the status of women in many cultures, the abolition of slavery, the promotion of education, agriculture, and medical care (294.1).

In the process, however, they largely overlooked the wise and beautiful side of non-Western cultures. They failed to appreciate "the unity of living and learning; the interdependence between individual, community, culture, and industry;

the profundity of folk wisdom; the proprieties of traditional societies. All these were swept aside by a mentality shaped by the Enlightenment which tended to turn people into objects, reshaping the entire world into the image of the West, separating humans from nature and from one another, and 'developing' them according to Western standards and suppositions" (294.7). In other words, it was the Enlightenment and not the gospel that made Western Christians so unappreciative of other cultures and so domineering over them. This has major implications for our later discussion of inculturation.

One key part of Western culture that was exported unthinkingly was the organizational structure of a church, including the employment of professional clergy. The unintended effect of this was, "Western mission agencies taught their converts to feel helpless without money" (296.1). The emerging churches were trapped. They had neither the financial base to support a church modeled on Western organizations nor the freedom from Western control that would have allowed them to develop a model of church they could afford.

6. The "manifest destiny" of Western nations (298.6)

The close ties between the gospel and Western culture had political implications which we will consider in this section on manifest destiny and the next on colonialism. "Manifest destiny" was "the conviction that God, in his providence, had chosen the Western nations, because of their unique qualities, to be the standard-bearers of his cause even to the uttermost ends of the world" (298.7). "Manifest" means obvious, unquestionable, as plain as the nose on your face.

Often but not always the destiny was thought to include the establishment of colonies (298.8), as we will see in point 7 below. Invariably the idea of a "manifest destiny" was nationalistic. The American destiny was "manifest" to the Americans, the British destiny to the British, and so on among the French, Germans, Dutch, Russians, and Afrikaners (299.6). For example, the English Puritans who settled New England "believed that the Anglo-Saxon race was divinely mandated to guide history to its end and usher in the millennium" (300.3).

The high point for manifest destiny thinking was approximately 1880–1915, when unprecedented technological marvels were unfolded in the West (electricity, telephone, telegraph, the Eiffel Tower, the airplane), political control of most of the world was very stable, and international trade was booming. At that time the Christian establishment and the political establishment were thoroughly enchanted with each other, at least in Britain and America. It seemed "manifest" to everyone that the Enlightenment (in science though not in philosophy) was a new God-given ship in which the gospel of Jesus Christ could sail the seven seas, touching and transforming societies in every port of call.

7. Colonialism (302.8)

As mentioned above, the idea of manifest destiny often played out as colonialism. "Modern missions originated in the context of modern Western colonialism" among Spanish and Portuguese Catholics in the sixteenth century and among Protestants, especially the British and Dutch, in the seventeenth (303.1).

The Spanish and Portuguese pattern, in which the government was the protagonist, was to establish political control of a territory from the beginning as the basis for trade and evangelization of the local people. The British and Dutch pattern, in which the trading companies were the protagonists, was to establish trading posts and invite the parent government to establish political control later if needed to protect trade and traders.

The Spanish and Portuguese governments built missionaries into their pattern of colonization; the British and Dutch trading companies at first prohibited missionaries because they could disrupt economic interaction with local residents and criticize the trading company to its parent government (303.7). As one colonial governor said, "What we want is to prepare the indigenous population for manual labor; you [missionaries] turn them into *people*" (311.3).

The relationship of missionaries to colonial powers has long been debated. Were they primarily friends and advocates for the local people victimized by colonization (311.5) or "ideal allies" of the colonial governments, the velvet glove that caused the local peoples to tolerate the iron fist of colonialism (303.8)? There is plenty of evidence on both sides.

On the positive side, there were missionaries like Las Casas who against all odds championed the rights of the oppressed (310.9). The Americans prided themselves on staying out of the colony business altogether (301.5). The Germans stayed out for a long time, arguing that "mission and colonialism are as far apart from one another as *heaven* and *earth*" (311.8). In nineteenth-century Britain, pressure both from missionaries and Christians at home caused the government to adopt policies of "benevolent colonialism." They began taking responsibility for the welfare of the colonized and tying the greedy hands of the trading companies, at least to some extent (307.2).

On the other hand, mission advocates sometimes wrote of collaboration with the state in terms that send shudders down the spine of a reader today: "The state may indeed incorporate the protectorates outwardly; it is however, the mission which must assist in securing the deeper aim of colonial policy, the inner colonization" (306.2, quoting Schmidlin).[5] Even the missionaries who did not cave in to colonialism "assumed, virtually without question, that colonialism was an inexorable force and that all they were required to do was somehow to try to tame it" (312.3).

The impact of colonialism on mission increased as the colonial system became more entrenched. It was reinforced in Britain by an upward shift in the social class of the missionary pool. Like William Carey, most British missionaries came from working-class backgrounds until the late nineteenth century. At that time there was a huge and highly successful movement to recruit missionaries from the

---

5. The term "inner colonization" is Bosch's translation from a German work of 1913. Fortunately it never came into common use in English missiological writing, but a similar formula did. The "three C's" of colonialism were "Christianity, commerce, and civilization," commonly assumed to be a package deal (305.8).

ranks of university-educated "gentlemen." While the missionaries from humble backgrounds had often seen themselves as the peers or even the servants of the people among whom they worked, "the new [university-educated] missionary force, conscious of its assets and imbued with the desire to save the world, as a matter of course took charge wherever it went" (307.8).

The step upward in social class turned out to be a step backward in mission. As we noted in point 2 above, the motivation of Jesus' love was transformed into a motivation of pity and condescension. Enlightened Christian missionaries were "the guardians of the less-developed races" (308.1).

Anthropological Motives

8. Voluntarism (327.5)

The formation of missionary societies inside and outside of denominational structures was a hallmark of this era of mission. "The spirit of enterprise and initiative spawned by the Enlightenment played an important role" in these efforts (327.9). William Carey's model for a mission society came not from the Bible or theology but from a type of business organization that developed during the Enlightenment — the overseas trading company (330.5).

The discovery that "like-minded individuals could band together in order to promote a common cause" followed logically from the Reformation and the Enlightenment (328.3). If each person may read Scripture for herself (as the Reformation insisted) and each person may think for herself (as the Enlightenment insisted), then each person must also be free to create or join any association for any reasonable, Scripture-based purpose that concerns her.

In their early days, these voluntary missionary societies focused on the concern of converting individuals, with little attention to the matter of organizing the converts into churches (331.7). In the mid-nineteenth century, Henry Venn and Rufus Anderson tried to correct this weakness by suggesting what kind of churches should be organized — self-supporting, self-governing, self-propagating (331.8). Later as the high imperial age of mission arrived, each denomination began to carve out its own territory and create a local church in its own image, even if still giving lip service to the famous "three-self formula."

At this same time, but in a part of the world that was not colonized (China's interior), Hudson Taylor pioneered a new type of voluntary society, the "faith mission." Taylor got away from the Europeans (including the missionaries) in the coastal cities, abandoned the "mission station" model in favor of living among the people, avoided denominational distinctives, and took the political control of the mission society along with him to China. In spite of some now well-known weaknesses such as a romantic notion of individual choices of converts, little interest in the social implications of the gospel, and a strong reliance on the charisma of the founder, the faith mission model came to play a major role in mission in the twentieth century (333.5).

9. *Missionary fervor, optimism, and pragmatism (334.3)*

In 1889 the emerging Student Volunteer Movement adopted its famous watch-word, "The evangelization of the world in this generation...." "More than anything else, it epitomized the Protestant missionary mood of the period: prag-matic, purposeful, activist, impatient, self-confident, single-minded, triumphant" (336.3). This was not the first time Americans had thought the whole world was in their reach. Already in 1818 Gordon Hall and Samuel Newell had published a book in which they suggested that the Western church could convert the world within twenty years (335.7).

By the end of the nineteenth century, it seemed that this was an idea whose time had come. "The hand of God in opening door after door among the nations of mankind, in unlocking the secrets of nature and in bringing to light invention after invention, is beckoning the Church of our day to larger achievements.... It seems entirely possible to fill the earth with the knowledge of Christ before the present generation passes away.... Ours is an age of unparalleled opportunity," wrote John R. Mott (338.1).

The "all-time highwater mark in Western missionary enthusiasm" was still to come (338.5). In 1910 the Edinburgh conference assumed that the final victory of Christian mission was just around the corner. There were more missionaries in more places reporting more success stories than ever before. With just a little more planning and cooperation among the many agencies, the mission could surely be accomplished. Four years later World War I derailed many of these naïve hopes as "Christian" nations fought each other to the death. Optimism about mission evaporated.

CONCLUSION

"Looking back at the many and varied motifs discussed in this chapter, one cannot help feeling overwhelmed. No single motif appeared to have dominated" (341.9). All the motives for mission, however, were shaped to a consider-able extent by Enlightenment assumptions, especially the "assured victory of progress.... There was a widespread and practically unchallengeable confidence in the ability of Western Christians to offer a cure-all for the ills of the world and guarantee progress to all — whether through the spread of 'knowledge' or 'the gospel' " (342.9).

The Enlightenment split the world into this-worldly and other-worldly levels ("fact" and "value," respectively). One form of Christianity (amillennialism) began to say that true religion dealt only with this world while another form (premillennialism) began to say that religion dealt only with the salvation of souls for the other-worldly level (343.2).

The impact of the Enlightenment on Christian mission was not only nega-tive (344.5). Its combination of attitudes, inventions, and explorations led many courageous, dedicated, and loving people to enter missionary service and take the gospel to all corners of the world. Of course, they were children of their time. Our problem is that to a considerable extent we are still children of their time, and the times are changing around us.

YOUR VIEWS AND YOUR CONTEXT

38. Write a theological critique of any one of the five threads of the Enlightenment worldview that appears to you to be seriously un-Christian. If none appear un-Christian, choose one and support it from a Christian theological stance.

39. From the table of four worldviews (Table 7, p. 70), choose the one you think is most defensible theologically or draw an alternative you think is better than any of them. Explain your thinking.

40. In retrospect the tight link between Christianity and Western "civilization" in the colonial era is seen as a serious mistake by almost everyone. How are the effects of that old link still visible in the church in your country? Is it possible to make a similar mistake in the future by linking Christianity too closely with civilizations that are not Western?

41. From the list of nine motives for mission after the Enlightenment, choose one you think is rightly emphasized by your church today, one that should be emphasized more than it is, and one that is leading (or tempting) your church to engage in mission for the wrong reason. Briefly give reasons for your choices.

42. In your personal opinion, did the Enlightenment have a net positive effect on the church and its mission, a net negative effect, or neither (with the positives and negatives basically canceling each other out)?

43. Write a prayer for your church based on the things you have realized about the impact of the Enlightenment on its theology and mission.

Table 8
Summary of Some Models of Mission in Church History

	Theme (and text)	Aspect of church	Some strengths	Some weaknesses	Complexities in the period[1]
Eastern Orthodoxy	Life and love (Jn. 3:16)	Worship	Affirmed the importance of life in this world, Affirmed the church as God's community	Lost its sense of urgency and much of its sense of mission, Got mired in philosophy	Illegal till 312, then official
Medieval Catholic	Filling the master's house (Lk. 14:23)	Structural authority	Attempted to create a Christian society and to require kings to act like followers of Jesus, Monks were model servants	Politicized its mission and rationalized violence, Focused on other-worldly salvation	Theological framework of Augustine or Aquinas
Reformation Protestant	Justification by faith (Ro. 1:16-17)	The Word	Rediscovery of God as a gracious missionary God, Emphasis on the Bible as central in Christian life	Church unity was lost; No emphasis on taking the gospel to non-Christian areas	Prot. Orthodoxy vs. Anabaptists, Pietists & Puritans
Modern era (Prot. & Cath.)	Saving the world (Lk. 4:18-19; Mt. 28:18-20)	Geograph- ical spread	Made Christianity global; Much sacrificial service	Western imperialism in theology, church and culture	Ecumenical vs. evangelical

[1] The drastic differences between movements within a period make it hard to generalize about each period as a whole as this table does. Bosch goes into these differences somewhat for the Reformation and modern periods but only touches on them for the other two eras.

PART THREE

AN EMERGING PARADIGM

Chapter 10

The Enlightenment Worldview Unraveling

(Bosch, TM, pp. 349–62)

In our day the Enlightenment explanation of life is coming apart at the seams. The unraveling started, quite ironically, in the very field of science that the Enlightenment considered its stronghold — physics. Einstein, Bohr, and Heisenberg put forward theories that shook the foundations of reason and of knowing (350.6). Two world wars in the twentieth century convinced humanity that the prevailing view of life, the Enlightenment view, could not be the best thing for the human race (350.7). As early as 1950, Guardini wrote that the modern era and the entire worldview on which it was based were collapsing (350.9). Polanyi and Kuhn went on to spell out the implications for the meaning of reason, knowledge, and science (351.4).

Let us look again at the five threads of Enlightenment thought described in the previous chapter to see how each one is disintegrating and how Christian mission may respond.

Thread 1. The Enlightenment put all its hope in reason, then restricted reason to the data provided by the five senses. "The narrow Enlightenment perception of rationality has, at long last, been found to be an inadequate cornerstone on which to build one's life" (352.9). The Enlightenment was supposed to open up infinite possibilities for humanity; instead it "stunted human growth" (353.1). People today want reason to have room for less precise but equally real ways of thinking and knowing, such as metaphor, myth, and analogy. They especially want a rationality that has room for their experience, including their spiritual experience (353.8). Christian mission is not a mission that explains everything but includes some things that remain beyond explanation.

Thread 2. The view of nature as a machine to study was supposed to liberate humans by giving them control over nature; instead it has enslaved humans and ruined nature (355.1). Humans have become production units, slaves to the global technological system. Nature seems to be heading into a long slide from the melting of the polar ice caps to the burning of the rain forests, with vast air and water pollution almost everywhere in between. Christian mission needs to affirm that people are not objects, technology is not God, and nature is not property.

Thread 3. The Enlightenment's focus on causes and effects rather than purpose "ultimately rendered the universe meaningless" (355.8). This was not noticed for a couple of centuries in Europe and North America, where the age of mechanization and colonization seemed to be bringing "progress" on all fronts. But eventually human beings, being human, insisted on meaning for their lives. They also came to believe that the most desirable future might not be the one humans can engineer. The Christian faith affirms a future that is breaking in on us at God's initiative rather than our planning. Christianity also affirms that repentance, conversion, and forgiveness are possible here and now even though they defy all normal laws of cause and effect (356.4).

Thread 4. The human race, which the Enlightenment absolutely trusted as savior of the world, eventually let the Enlightenment down. Even in the mid-twentieth century, when human power and technology had reached levels unimaginable to previous generations, the application of it all to the "development" of the Third World was a failure, even a fiasco. "Development was not...a new word for peace, but another word for exploitation" (357.9). One of the Christian responses to this breakdown was liberation theology, which insisted that human beings could not be trusted — at least not the ones holding wealth and power (358.3). Postmodernism has adopted this view.

Thread 5. Belief in "value-free" objective knowledge went together with Threads 3 and 4 above (loss of meaning; trust in humans) to open the door for the planetary curses of the twentieth century — the great ideologies of Marxism, Capitalism, Fascism, and Nazism. "It belongs to the nature of ideology to parade itself in the guise of science and to appeal to objective reason" (359.4). The irony of this pseudo-science is intense and it is crucial for understanding our world. When an ideology refuses to admit that it is partly based on its own commitment rather than purely on objective facts, it becomes "the Big Lie" because it can neither critique itself nor allow anyone else to do so (360.3). It is the perfect formula for tyranny. "A post-Enlightenment self-critical Christian stance may, in the modern world, be the only means of neutralizing the ideologies; it is the only vehicle that can save us from self-deception and free us from dependence on utopian dreams" (361.2).

   In light of the disintegration of the threads that held the Enlightenment paradigm together and the devastation caused by Enlightenment-based ideologies, there is a strong cynical streak in postmodern thought today. Many who have given up on the Enlightenment are also giving up on all grand integrative dreams ("metanarratives") that claim to lead humanity together into a better future. There is no hope for the world.

Or is there? The road that beckons the truly enlightened in our time is "a road beyond Enlightenment optimism and anti-Enlightenment pessimism" (362.1). It is the road we cannot yet see clearly, but we will sketch it as far as we can in the next two chapters. At least we know which road it is — the road of Christian mission.

It may lead us to a place where Christianity does not serve a "religious" function in the religious box where the Enlightenment says religions belong, the box of "values and opinions." Instead this kind of Christianity will be outside the box. It will point not only toward religious salvation but also toward the actual solution of human problems in this world, just like all the grand, failed post-Enlightenment ideologies did. However, it will not be an ideology because it will not be driven to impose any final, absolutely reasonable solution on the wider world. By Enlightenment standards, it will be neither a religion nor an ideology. It will be an unimaginable hybrid of the two without becoming a religious ideology or an ideological religion. It will be an altogether different sort of thing, the sort that no one but God could dream up. Let us take a closer look.

YOUR VIEWS AND YOUR CONTEXT

44. Agree or disagree: The unraveling of the Enlightenment worldview is mostly a Western problem. It has a few implications for mission in the many parts of the world where the Enlightenment never had decisive influence over the culture.

45. Explain in your own words what Bosch means by this statement: "A post-Enlightenment self-critical Christian stance may, in the modern world, be the only means of neutralizing the ideologies." What ideology or ideologies are the most tempting ones in your society today and how would such a "Christian stance" neutralize them?

Chapter 11

Church and Mission in Flux

(Bosch, TM, pp. 363–67)

The previous chapter explained, "It is becoming increasingly evident that the modern gods of the West — science, technology, and industrialization — have lost their magic" (363.5). The world is no longer spellbound by these three "gods," and it is losing confidence in the saving power of all three.

The world in which we do our mission has changed, but so have we, the church. The church has been diversified and enriched as theological themes long absent have been rediscovered by various small movements and then integrated into mainstream Christianity: the vivid expectation of Christ's return, the gifts of the Spirit, the importance of the laity and of personal decisions of Christian commitment, and the refusal to identify with the state in violence and war (363.8). The church has also lost its position of privilege in society, begun dialogue with the religions and sects it used to condemn, and built bridges among its denominations (364.3).

The position of Western mission agencies and missionaries has shifted. Many countries no longer admit Christian missionaries. Where missionaries go to work with "younger churches," they are seen as fraternal workers who are perhaps useful but "not central to the life and future of the younger churches" (364.9).

Missionaries have fallen from the super-spiritual pedestal that had held them above criticism for over a century. The many strategic and moral mistakes of previous generations of missionaries are now being recognized and acknowledged. Even a writer very sympathetic to mission concludes that missionaries "have on the whole been a feeble folk, not very wise, not very holy, not very patient. They have broken most of the commandments and fallen into every conceivable mistake" (365.4, quoting Neill).

Today in the church and in mission there is plenty of change to cope with and plenty of mistakes to repent of. "Repentance has to begin with a bold recognition of the fact that the church-in-mission is today facing a world fundamentally different from anything it faced before. This in itself calls for a new understanding of mission" (366.1).

"The thesis of this study is that in the field of religion, a paradigm shift always means both continuity and change, both faithfulness to the past and boldness to engage the future, both constancy and contingency, both tradition and transformation" (366.3). The key to a new paradigm for mission will be "creative tension" between these apparent opposites (367.5), just as it has been in all the paradigm changes we have reviewed so far. Let us attempt to sketch a new paradigm for mission seeing how creative we can be and how much tension we can handle.

YOUR VIEWS AND YOUR CONTEXT

46. How is the challenge of mission in your country different today than it was a century ago? How is it the same?

47. How is the challenge of mission in your country different today than it was a decade or two ago? How is it the same?

Chapter 12

Elements of an Emerging Paradigm of Mission

(Bosch, TM, pp. 368–510)

The interweaving of church and mission is the integrating theme of the thirteen overlapping components of the new paradigm of mission. These may be grouped under six headings as follows:[1]

A. The **source** of mission — *missio Dei* (389.6–393.1)

B. The **goals** of mission — salvation (393.2–400.8), justice (400.9–408.9)

C. The **activities** of mission — evangelism (409.1–420.8), contextualization (420.9–457.5, including liberation and inculturation)

D. The **bearer** of mission[2] — the whole church (368.7–389.5), ecumenism (457.6–467.4), laity (467.5–474.5)

E. The **limits** of mission — its "witness" nature (474.6–489.6), its time frame (498.9–510.5)

F. The **study** of mission — missiology and theology (489.7–498.8)

---

1. Warning: Bosch does not outline his paradigm in this way and he might have been unhappy to see me attempt it. The danger is that my six categories will be tidier than the complex reality I am trying to describe. I am taking the risk of making an outline anyway because many of the rest of us, unlike Bosch, simply cannot hold this many dimensions of a paradigm in our heads and do anything useful with them unless we have some categories as handles. Bosch's outline of his paradigm (368–510) has thirteen (unnumbered) sections. I have reduced these to six by grouping and rearranging the topics as shown in the box above .

2. Concerning the dangers in the term "bearer of mission," see note 7 on p. 115.

Figure 4 (p. 94) shows the first five of these aspects of mission, numbered according to the key at the upper left. It is an attempt to summarize Bosch's chapter 12 (143 pages!) in one page.[3] Note the following features of the diagram:

1. The diagram flows from left to right, starting with the heart of God at the time of creation and ending at the eschaton when God's mission will be accomplished. The timeline at the bottom shows the stages which correspond to the parts of the diagram above them.

2. The goal of God's mission is a just and saved universe. The two overlapping circles at the right show that justice and salvation are intertwined parts of one reality. Neither is a substitute for the other. Neither is meant to stand on its own.

3. The central thrust of God's mission is what creates the church. That central thrust used to consist of the Covenant and the Law given to Israel through Moses at Sinai. Since the coming of Jesus the Messiah, it consists of two main activities — evangelism and contextualization. Contextualization may be subdivided into liberation and inculturation.

4. The relation of mission to the church is similar to the relationship of an arrow to the line that represents the outer edge of the arrow's shape. The reality is the shape, not the edge, but the real shape cannot be seen if there is no edge. The church thus "draws" God's mission, making it visible to the world.

5. The vertical arrows from the church to the world around it ("Other faiths and isms" and "History and cultures") represent the church's interaction with that world. This is most commonly referred to as "dialogue" with other faiths and "engagement" in history. Suffering is part of the picture in both cases.

6. The mission of the church takes place only during the time between Christ's first coming to earth and his return (the two vertical rectangles). Before this there was no news to announce because the Messiah had not arrived. Afterward there will be no need to announce it because everyone will know it. The first rectangle cut mostly across the path of Israel; the second one will cut across all faiths and cultures.

---

3. Any diagram runs the risk of implying some wrong things while clarifying the right things. Some known weaknesses of the current diagram are these: (1) it appears that "Other faiths and isms" are completely separate from "History and cultures," which of course is not true. They are both part of "the world" in which the "church" exists. A three-dimensional model might show history and culture as a pipe with the church running through the middle rather than as two separate streams alongside the church. (2) The role of Israel appears to have terminated when the church began. This complete cancellation is not an adequate representation of Bosch's view of Israel. (3) Only one arrow goes between the church and "other faiths" and one between the church and "history." In fact, there could be many such arrows parallel to these because the engagement of the church and world happens continuously between Christ's first coming and his return. But many arrows would clutter the diagram too much and require still further explanation.

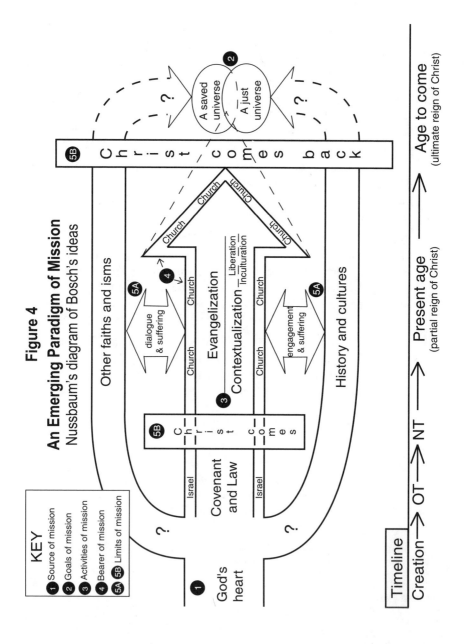

Figure 4
An Emerging Paradigm of Mission
Nussbaum's diagram of Bosch's ideas

7. Though the church is central to God's mission, it is not the whole story. Part of God's mission also flows through two other channels — "Other faiths and isms" and "History and culture." The question marks where the streams diverge indicate Bosch's uncertainty about how much of God's mission is going through those channels compared to the amount going straight ahead through Israel and the church. Similarly the question marks at the right end of these streams indicate ambiguity about the convergence of the streams once Christ comes back. Bosch does not want to say that all religions and particularly all ideologies lead ultimately to a just and saved universe, but neither does he want to exclude them entirely.

8. Three later diagrams are based on this one. The others show how this picture of mission is redrawn by traditional evangelicals, liberationists, and pluralists (Figures 5, 6, and 9, on pages 100, 101, and 127).

A. THE SOURCE OF MISSION
The *Missio Dei*
(Bosch, TM, pp. 389–93)

Let us begin with the source of mission, which closely relates to ownership. *Where does mission come from? Whose mission is it?*

Before the modern missionary era, the prevailing view was that "mission" in the sense of communicating the gospel to nations outside Christendom, was God's work. God would accomplish it "without your help or mine," as says the famous quote from a Baptist critic of William Carey in 1793. Carey was arguing that Western Christians should take some human initiative in mission — form missionary societies, raise money, send people. Over the next century and a half, people became so convinced of the importance of human initiative that they hardly thought of God as being active in mission. They only thought of human resources, human strategies, and human efforts.

To get God back into the mission picture and keep him there, Barth and some of his followers moved the theological basis for Christian mission from the doctrine of the church and the doctrine of salvation to the doctrine of the Trinity. "The classical doctrine on the *missio Dei* [mission of God] as God the Father sending the Son, and God the Father and the Son sending the Spirit was expanded to include yet another 'movement': Father, Son, and Holy Spirit sending the church into the world" (390.4).

"In the new image mission is not primarily an activity of the church, but an attribute of God. God is a missionary God.... Mission is thereby seen as a movement from God to the world; the church is viewed as an instrument for that mission.... To participate in mission is to participate in the movement of God's love toward people" (390.8).

"Mission has its origin in the heart of God. God is a fountain of sending love. This is the deepest source of mission. It is impossible to penetrate deeper still; there is mission because God loves people" (392.9).

When mission is recognized as *God's* mission and we see the Triune God as both the source and owner, at least three major implications follow:

1. Mission is bigger than the church, that is, God may work outside the church too. The church cannot be arrogant about its mission or itself.

2. The church is derived from mission, and not the other way around. Mission cannot be incidental to the life of the church.

3. Mission cannot be reduced to conversions and church membership. God has bigger, wider things in mind.

In the past half-century these points have come to be widely accepted and valued in both Protestant and Catholic circles. However, the term *missio Dei* itself has meanwhile backfired and now is of very limited usefulness because it has come to mean opposite things (392.3 and 392.8).

The devil is in the *"Dei."* For some, *"Dei"* came to mean God in a generic sense, the God of any and all religions, not the Father-Son-Spirit God of the New Testament. If *missio Dei* means the mission of the God/god of all religions, then the only proper "mission" of Christians is to dialogue with others among whom God is also presumed to be working. On the other hand, if *Dei* means the Triune God, then Christian mission must have at its core a witness to the Son in the power of the Spirit. The contrast between these two views is perhaps the decisive watershed in current missiology,[4] yet both sides are still using the same term, *missio Dei,* for their contradictory purposes. We will look at this issue in more detail in section E (pp. 124–33 below) on other religions.

YOUR VIEWS AND YOUR CONTEXT

48. Barth talked of three sendings: the Father sending the Son, the Father and the Son sending the Spirit, and the Father-Son-Spirit sending the church. How is that view of the church as "phase three in the mission of God" different from the view of the church held by most ordinary members of your church?

49. Which of the three implications of recognizing God as the source and owner of mission most needs discussion in your church or mission and why?

50. What would it mean to "derive mission from church" rather than to "derive church from mission" as Bosch proposes? How important do you think it is to distinguish these two approaches to understanding church and mission?

---

4. See pp. 125–29 for further development of this idea.

B. THE GOALS OF MISSION
Salvation and Justice
(Bosch, TM, pp. 393–408)

Bringing salvation (393.1–400.8)

"For Christians, the conviction that God has decisively wrought salvation for all in and through Jesus Christ stands at the very center of their lives" (393.3). Naturally Christians want to make that salvation known and available to everyone. This salvation-sharing desire is "the throbbing heart of missiology" (393.4, quoting Gort). But what is "salvation"? Our answer to that not so simple question will determine the scope of our missionary activities (393.6).

Even in the New Testament we see that the concept of salvation is treated in a variety of ways by different writers. For example, Luke emphasizes salvation here and now (393.9) while Paul puts equal or greater emphasis on the future and final dimensions of salvation. In the centuries that followed, the Eastern church came to regard salvation as a gradual process (*theosis*) in which the believer was uplifted to become more God-filled and God-like (394.4). By contrast the Western church associated salvation with the one-time baptism into the death of Christ and the church's guarantee of salvation in the world to come.

When the Enlightenment came in the West, the church was regarded not as the bearer of salvation but as one of the things from which the world needed to be saved by the exercise of reason (395.5). The church responded to this challenge in two ways. The conservatives ignored it and continued to preach the necessity of salvation through the blood of Christ, reasonable or not. The liberals accepted the challenge and took out the parts of the Christian salvation message that looked unreasonable from the perspective of the Enlightenment. "Here not the *person* of Jesus was at the center but the *cause* of Jesus; the *ideal,* not the One who embodied the ideal; the *teaching* (particularly the Sermon on the Mount), not the Teacher; the *kingdom* of God, but without the King" (395.9).

The liberal, optimistic, and blood-free view of salvation was severely challenged by Barth from the 1920s to the 1950s, but in the 1960s and 1970s it had another spurt of life, perhaps a last gasp in light of the world situation today. The optimistic high point came at the 1973 conference of the World Council of Churches in Bangkok on the theme "Salvation Today," which defined salvation "exclusively in this-worldly terms" (396.9). Salvation is to be seen, inside or outside the church, in the struggle for economic justice, human dignity, human solidarity, and hope in personal life. Just two years later at the Nairobi Assembly of the World Council of Churches, a more sober view was already coming to the fore. "It was self-deception to begin to think and act as if salvation lay in our grasp, was at our disposal, or was something *we* could bring about" (397.7).[5]

---

5. This disillusionment with Christian "salvation" among liberals in the 1970s has steered many of them toward pluralism in the 1990s. They now seek salvation not within Christianity but in the new dialogue they propose among religions as equals.

The Enlightenment challenge thus still waits for a good Christian answer. The conservative answer was not believable for an "enlightened" world. The liberal answer turned out not to be believable even to the liberals themselves (399.3). To move beyond the former answers, we need to build a broader biblical base for our understanding of Jesus and on this base to build a broader understanding of salvation. The key to this is to realize that each of the views of salvation over the centuries has singled out and revolved around only one particular aspect of Jesus' life and ministry. The Eastern church focused on his incarnation, the Western church on his crucifixion, and the post-Enlightenment liberals on his teaching ministry.

Why not bring all these emphases, plus the resurrection and the return, together in a comprehensive picture of Christ that will carry us straight into a comprehensive picture of salvation?[6] "We should find a way *beyond* every schizophrenic position and minister to people in their *total* need,... we should involve individual as well as society, soul *and* body, present *and* future in our ministry of salvation" (399.8).

With this comprehensive view of salvation, Christians today should not — dare not — give up our mission of announcing salvation in Christ to the world and showing the world the preliminary effects of that salvation. "From the tension between the salvation *indicative* (salvation is already a reality!) and the salvation *subjunctive* (comprehensive salvation is yet to come!) there emerges the salvation *imperative* — Get involved in the ministry of salvation!" (400.7). This is our mission, not to establish his reign throughout the earth but to "erect bridgeheads" for it, anchored in the personal repentance and the faith commitment of people longing to welcome him (400.5).

The quest for justice (400.9–408.9)

The comprehensive view of salvation described in the previous section obviously includes justice, but narrower definitions of salvation have often been preached. "The relationship between the evangelistic and the societal dimensions of the Christian mission constitutes one of the thorniest areas in the theology and practice of mission" (401.1). For much of the twentieth century, justice issues were handled in opposite ways by ecumenicals and evangelicals. The result was two quite different paradigms of mission and a lot of hostility between their advocates.

In terms of our previous diagram of Bosch's "Emerging Paradigm of Mission," the ecumenicals focused on only one of the two circles representing the goal of mission (the "just universe" circle) while the evangelicals focused only on the other (the "saved universe" circle). The two following diagrams show the implications for an entire model of mission. The two models may be a useful

---

6. Bosch himself takes this approach in his final chapter, 512–18, sketching six aspects of Christology. For the summary see pp. 136–138 below.

reference point later in the chapter, especially in section C (pp. 104–15), where evangelism and contextualization are compared.

The traditional evangelical model (see Figure 5, p. 100) focuses on the goal of saved souls, that is, individuals who spend eternity in heaven rather than hell. The goal of mission is to get as many saved as possible and do it as soon as possible. The main activity of mission is therefore evangelization, announcing the good news of Jesus Christ and his saving sacrifice. Work for justice is fine but secondary because it does not contribute much toward the real goal of mission. The streams of "Other faiths and isms" and "History and cultures" have human and/or demonic origins; God has only a small bit of influence on them (dotted lines). The relation of the church to them is therefore mostly seen in terms of conflict. The church preaches at the other faiths and they oppose the church. The church does not engage very actively with "History and cultures" (note no down arrow to that stream). Instead a hostile secular world corrupts and persecutes the church.

A radical liberationist model (see Figure 6, p. 101) is almost the opposite of the traditional evangelical model. The goal of mission is a just world. Salvation in a religious or individual sense is not a significant issue. God's mission is simply to move the world toward justice. He is doing this primarily through historical processes, especially social, economic, political, and scientific processes. The main bearer of mission is history and cultures. The church, like other faiths and isms, is a side stream of God's mission, valuable to the extent that it aims in the same direction as historical processes. However, the church sometimes becomes an institution which harbors or even promotes injustice. At that point, the church must be rejected by the world so that God's mission may move ahead. Note that the two arrivals of the Messiah are both missing from this model. Many liberationists do not think Jesus himself worked aggressively enough for liberation (though some of his teaching is occasionally useful). They also fear that a belief in his literal return to earth may detract people from working for justice here and now.

Some of the contrasting features of the two models are shown in Table 9 (p. 102). The overall pattern was that ecumenicals tended to reduce mission to justice issues; evangelicals tended to see justice issues as incidental to mission.

One way the evangelicals described the relation of evangelism and justice was "to distinguish two different *mandates,* the one spiritual, the other social" (403.6). The evangelicals claimed two things: (1) the spiritual or evangelistic mandate would always take priority, and (2) the ecumenicals had been distracted from real mission (that is, spiritual mission) by the very secondary social mandate. The evangelicals were not saying that justice is unimportant but that they believed it would be the inevitable fruit of the spiritual conversion of individuals (404.9).

The polarization of the two views was worst in the 1920s (the Social Gospel heyday) and again in the "secular sixties" and early 1970s (402.8). Since the early 1980s there has been a general convergence on the justice issue among ecumenicals, Roman Catholics, and, somewhat surprisingly, evangelicals. By 1983

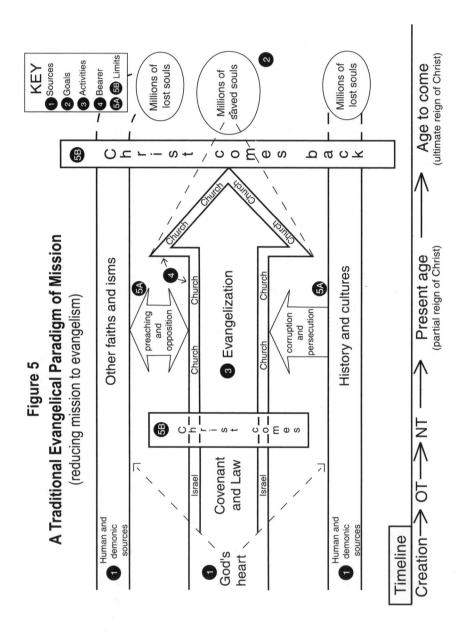

Figure 5
A Traditional Evangelical Paradigm of Mission
(reducing mission to evangelism)

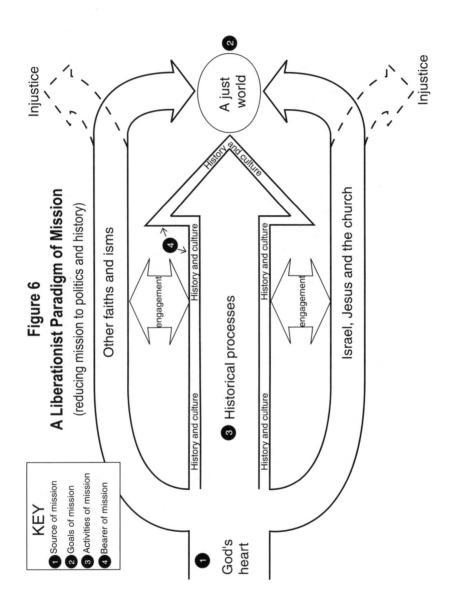

Figure 6
A Liberationist Paradigm of Mission
(reducing mission to politics and history)

KEY

1 Source of mission
2 Goals of mission
3 Activities of mission
4 Bearer of mission

Table 9
A Comparison of Ecumenicals and Evangelicals

	Ecumenical (prophetic emphasis; 402.6)	Evangelical (mystical emphasis; 402.6)
Theory	Justice the direct goal of mission	Justice the side effect of conversion
Location of evil	Social structures	Individual hearts
Goal	Social transformation	Individual conversions; church growth
Method	Church speaks out as an organization	Some Christians speak out as individuals
Value	Effective action for justice	Pure motives of love
Pattern	A "rational ethic"	A "religious ethic"
Historical precedent	Aquinas — harmony of upper and lower levels of reality	Augustine — contrast of bright heaven and dark world

evangelicals were making official conference statements such as, "Evil is not only in the human heart but also in social structures.... The mission of the church includes both the proclamation of the Gospel and its demonstration. We must therefore evangelize, respond to immediate human needs, and press for social transformation" (407.6). At about the same time, ecumenicals also began to get more explicit about God and the kingdom of God when they talked of their justice commitments. Justice rooted in God now seems to be on everyone's agenda.

Before leaving the subject, we must note that the methods of promoting justice as part of Christian mission have changed because of the Enlightenment. During the era of European Christendom (roughly 300–1800), political rulers had seen themselves as God-appointed. Church leaders therefore could expect them to listen to criticism from a biblical perspective on justice issues. The Enlightenment changed all that by breaking the link between church and state. Political rulers could no longer use the church as the foundation for their right to rule but neither could they any longer be held accountable by the church. For example, when a group of British bishops tried to intervene and speak for justice in a coal mining labor dispute in the 1920s, the prime minister asked how they would like it if he referred the revision of the Athanasian Creed to the Iron and Steel Federation (402.1)! Where today can the church corporately or Christians individually find a leg to stand on as they address the state about justice? We will consider some of the options in the sections on contextualization and liberation theology below.

YOUR VIEWS AND YOUR CONTEXT

51. The "salvation-sharing desire" which is the "throbbing heart of missiology" is not something one learns from a book. How would you describe the throbbing heart of missiology in your own words? Where and how did you learn it?

52. Compare and contrast an idea of salvation built around the person of Jesus with one built around the cause of Christ. How will the mission activities based on these two ideas differ?

53. Suppose you know one group of missionaries who sees its goal as "saving the world" and another group who sees its goal as "erecting bridgeheads for the world's salvation" (as Bosch puts it). What difference will it make in the way they go about their mission? Which group would you prefer to work with and why?

54. Write a short critique of the diagram of either the evangelical or the liberationist variation on Bosch's paradigm, whichever you think is the more important one for you to understand in your context. How fair and clear is the diagram? How might it be improved to more accurately describe the view of the evangelicals or the liberationists in your experience?

55. Choose one of the following aspects of Christology that is most important in your own theology of mission (incarnation, teaching ministry, crucifixion, resurrection, return). What primary goal of mission and what main mission activity or activities are implied by your choice?

56. Choose either of these questions:

    (a) Which of the models of church-state relationships that we have observed from the New Testament to today is the most promising basis for mission in your country/region in the new era of mission and why?

    (b) Is it any more appropriate for church bishops to speak to the government about justice for coal miners than (as in the example Bosch cites) for the government to send the Iron and Steel Federation to advise the church about its theology? Explain your reasoning.

57. In your situation what signs are there of a convergence of evangelicals and ecumenicals around justice issues? How, if at all, do the two camps still differ?

C. THE ACTIVITIES OF MISSION
Evangelism and Contextualization
(Bosch, TM, pp. 409–57)

Evangelism (409.1–420.9)

The relation of the terms "mission" and "evangelism" has become terribly confused in our day, as shown in Table 10. The Bible does not help us sort this situation out because the term "mission" is barely there while "evangelizing" (Greek, *euangelizein*) and its derivatives are frequent. To make matters worse, English Bible translators rarely say, "Jesus was evangelizing in the villages." They say he was "preaching the gospel" (409.3).

Evangelism is best seen as a subset of mission. "Mission denotes the total task God has set the church.... Mission is the church sent into the world, to love, to serve, to preach, to teach, to heal, to liberate" (412.1). Evangelism is the preaching-teaching part of this. It is "our opening up of the mystery of God's love to all people inside that mission" (412.5, quoting Castro).

Evangelism is an announcement

"Evangelism is announcing that God, Creator and Lord of the universe, has personally intervened in human history and has done so supremely through the

Table 10
Some Definitions of Mission and Evangelism

	"Mission"	"Evangelism"/"Evangelization"
RC & ecumenicals	To people who have never been Christian	To lapsed "Christians"
Evangelicals	(avoid term as too generic)	The core part of "mission," i.e., preaching the gospel
1950-80, widespread	Same as evangelism	Same as mission
RC & ecumenicals in 80s	(avoid term as colonialist)	Replace the term "mission" as the label for everything the church says or does in the world

person and ministry of Jesus of Nazareth who is the Lord of history, Savior and Liberator. In this Jesus, incarnate, crucified, and risen, the reign of God has been inaugurated" (412.8).

Since evangelism is basically an announcement (a piece of news) about God's activity, it is always connected to the *missio Dei.* We could say it informs people of the new stage that the *missio Dei* has entered. The newsy nature of the gospel has at least four implications:

1. Words are required. "This message [of the arriving kingdom and king] is indeed necessary. It is unique. It cannot be replaced [by unexplained deeds]" (413.9, quoting *Evangelii Nuntiandi*).

2. Words must be backed up by lifestyle and action. If the arriving king has no impact on his followers, why should anyone else pay attention to them when they announce he is here? (414.1). If their lives are unchanged (unconverted), how can they call others to "conversion"?

3. Church membership cannot be the primary aim of the announcement. At its heart, the gospel is news about God's action and his reign, not his institution. Evangelical leaders, especially in the Church Growth school of thought, and Roman Catholics have often taken the mistaken view that the success of mission correlates directly to church membership growth (415.3).

4. There is no perfect set of words that captures the gospel. "We may never limit the gospel to our understanding of God and of salvation. We can only witness in humble boldness and bold humility to our understanding of that gospel" (420.4).

The announcement calls for a personal response

If a king walks into a room, his presence demands a response from anyone and everyone in that room. They cannot pretend that nothing has happened and go on with whatever they were doing before. The gospel announcement is like that. Jesus says, "Repent, and believe the gospel" (413.2, quoting Mark 1:15).

Repentance (Greek, *metanoia,* "turning" or "changing of the mind") "involves a turning *from* and a turning *to*" — "*from* a life characterized by sin, separation from God, submission to evil, and the unfulfilled potential of God's image, *to* a new life characterized by the forgiveness of sins, obedience, . . . renewed fellowship with God" (413.3, quoting *Mission and Evangelism*). The gospel is "the announcement of a personal encounter, mediated by the Holy Spirit, with the living Christ, receiving his forgiveness and making a personal acceptance of the call to discipleship" (416.4, quoting *Mission and Evangelism*). The personal nature of the response has several implications:

1. "Principalities and powers, governments and nations cannot come to faith —
   only individuals can" (416.7). Making prophetic statements to governments
   may be mission but it is not evangelism, for evangelism is always addressed
   to persons.

2. The personal response cannot stay on the religious surface of a person's
   life. It has to penetrate all the way down to the core of a person's being,
   uncomfortable as that may be. It cannot be motivated by social respectability, upward mobility, or cultural conformity. It cannot aim "at satisfying
   rather than transforming people" (417.5). Granted, the gospel does come
   as peace and comfort to people in tragedy and emptiness, "but only within
   the context of it being a word about the lordship of Christ in all realms of
   life" (417.9).

3. The personal response is an enlistment for service. "Jesus' invitation to
   people to follow him and become his disciples is asking people whom they
   want to serve. Evangelism is, therefore, a call to *service*" (418.3). "To win
   people to Jesus is to win their allegiance to God's priorities. . . . Evangelism,
   then, is calling people to mission" (418.7).

The personal response must be free and authentic

Back to our picture of a king entering a room. People may respond to his
arrival in a variety of ways. They may respectfully welcome him. If they have
never seen him before, they may question whether he is the king he claims to be.
They may ignore him or even reject him, though this could be dangerous.

The heralds of the king, however, do not precede him into the room to read
a list of all the terrible things he will do to those who do not properly welcome
him. Their emphasis is on the good news that he is arriving. They are informing
people and inviting them to welcome him. "Evangelism is always invitation"
(413.5). It is not a matter of coaxing people or threatening them but, as a matter
of common courtesy, joyfully letting them know what is about to happen so they
can share in it.

Those who decide to welcome the king become part of the church — the
fellowship of king-welcomers. To disregard the church as some "Christians" were
doing in the 1960s is "totally inappropriate. Without the church there can be no
evangelism or mission" (416.2).

The king brings present salvation and the assurance of eternal bliss, which of
course are powerful reasons to welcome him gladly. "However, if the offer of
all this gets center-stage attention in our evangelism, the gospel is degraded to a
consumer product. It has to be emphasized, therefore, that the personal enjoyment
of salvation never becomes the central theme in biblical conversion stories. . . . It
is not simply to *receive* life that people are called to become Christians, but rather
to *give* life" (414.7).

Summary

Evangelism is "that dimension and activity of the church's mission which, by word and deed and in the light of particular conditions and a particular context, offers every person and community, everywhere, a valid opportunity to be directly challenged to a radical reorientation of their lives" (420.7).

The reorientation involves such things as:

- Deliverance from slavery to the world and its powers
- Embracing Christ as Savior and Lord
- Becoming a living member of Christ's community, the church
- Being enlisted into his service of reconciliation, peace, and justice on earth
- Being committed to God's purpose of placing all things under the rule of Christ (420.8)

Contextualization (420.9–457.5)

"A basic argument of this book has been that, from the very beginning, the missionary message of the Christian church incarnated itself in the life and world of those who had embraced it. It is, however, only fairly recently that this essentially contextual nature of the faith has been recognized" (421.4). The prevailing Western opinion for the past two centuries of mission has been just the opposite. Western Christians "simply assumed that [their theology] was supracultural and universally valid" (448.6), just as people who grow up in the middle of the United States assume that people from their region are the only ones who speak English without an accent.

Today we realize that mission in the colonial era had a very thick Western accent and that the gospel must be reformulated (contextualized) so it comes through to local people with a local accent. As we will see, contextualization goes far deeper than the superficial levels of culture such as the clothing of the clergy or the style of music used in worship.

The foundations for a contextual approach to theology were laid by Schleiermacher in the early nineteenth century, starting from the premise that every text (including biblical texts) was affected by the total context (*Sitz im leben*) in which it was written (422.8). The goal of biblical scholarship was to identify these contexts so that the scholar could discount the unnecessary or unsound influences on the text and explain for current readers the true, deeper or "real" meaning of the text for today. One of the clearest examples of this procedure in the twentieth century was Bultmann's attempt to "demythologize" the New Testament, taking out the "myths" (such as miracles) that "Enlightened" people could not believe.

A major problem with this approach, which dominated theology for nearly two centuries, was that the Western theologians who were using it "did not realize that their own interpretations were as parochial and as conditioned by their context as those they were criticizing" (423.1). They were trying to remove the cultural splinter from the eye of the biblical writers without taking into account the cultural plank in their own eyes.

The breakthrough came in the 1960s when theologians from the Third World began to write from their own cultural perspectives — liberation theology, black theology, feminist theology, etc. (423.6). They claimed that the proper quest of theology is not the quest for universal truths that float ideally above history; it is the quest for acting properly in a real, local situation that is infested by evil in a particular way. The first "step" in theology is therefore not a theoretical question such as "What is God like?" but a practical commitment to the poor and marginalized. Having made that commitment, a theologian begins dealing with a practical question: "How should a Christian act to get rid of the oppressive evil in this situation?" This in turn begs a theoretical question: "What is wrong here? Exactly where is the evil in this situation, and how does its oppressive force work?"

In contextualized theology these practical and theoretical questions are so closely linked to each other and to the local situation that theological answers to them will never produce a final, universal theology (427.7; though a few contextualizers have tried to impose their theology across cultural lines, 428.6). Instead, each theological statement is seen as part of an experimental process, a "hermeneutical circle" moving from praxis or experience to theological reflection to praxis to reflection, and so on, all with the aim of transforming history (425.1).

Western theology is rightly criticized because it does not share this aim. Western theologians generally think and write as if knowing, understanding, and explaining are the only valid aims of theology. They rarely get their hands dirty in history, taking the side of the poor and experiencing life from their perspective. They are implying, if not actually saying, that this Western-dominated, oppressive world is basically legitimate. This is repulsive to theologians who are able to see things through the pain-glazed eyes of the poor (424.3).

A critique of the contextualized approach to theology

We must begin by recognizing the rock-solid theological foundations of the arguments of the contextualizers.

- God is interested in this world he created; an other-worldly theology cannot be true to the true God (426.1).

- God gets involved with the world, taking the side of victims and opposing their oppressors; a theology that is a bystander in the battle of oppressed and oppressors cannot be true to God (425.9).

- As God incarnate, Jesus became a part of the world; a theology that stands apart from the world reopens the very gap between God and humanity that Jesus came to close (426.7).

- Jesus "immersed himself in the altogether real circumstances of the poor, the captives, the blind, the oppressed" (Luke 4:18f; 426.3); a theology that remains academic and detached from the concerns of the poor is not a theology that follows Jesus.

- The resurrected Jesus "propels human history toward the end," making everything new (Rev. 21:5; 426.4); a theology that detaches religion from history detaches it from the Messiah, the hope of history.

These foundations in the past, present, and future give contextualization a firm place to stand within the emerging paradigm of mission. Since contextualization will be such an important part of the future of mission, we must learn to handle it well, avoiding some of the pitfalls that a few decades of experience have already revealed.

- When we take history seriously, we may take it too seriously and neglect the religious side of life. We may focus exclusively on social and political issues, assuming that everything God does, he does through historical processes. We may forget that God speaks as an independent being, and not always in ways we would expect (426.7).

- When we read the signs of the times in history, we may misread them. We may suppose, as many Christians did at the time, that certain developments such as the rise of Nazism or the revolution against the white regime in Zimbabwe were entirely God's work, his perfect solution for their national problems (429.1). "Compassion and commitment, apparently, are no guarantee that one will not produce bad sociology, practice poor politics, and pursue debatable historical analysis" (429.5).

- When we center on praxis rather than theory, we may forget "that there is no praxis without theory, even where the theory is not spelled out" (431.3). Theory (a truth concern, a matter of faith) and praxis (a justice concern, a matter of hope) need to be balanced with "poesis," the imaginative use of images (a beauty concern, a matter of love; 431.7).

- When we insist on a different theology to fit each local context, we run the risk of relativism. We may forget that we have any connection with or accountability to the global body of Christ. We trust ourselves and our local theology completely (427.7).

Ironically, all these risks are really forms of taking Western theology too seriously. While reacting to it, some contextualizers overreact. They define their position more in contrast to Western theology than in harmony with biblical theology. By recognizing the risks of such a reactionary form of contextualization, we may pursue the contextual approach to theology wisely. We might not take the risks if Western theology were risk-free, but that is clearly not the case. Let us turn then to two prominent forms of contextualization — liberation theology and inculturation.

Liberation theology

"Theologies of liberation, particularly the classical Latin American variety, evolved in protest against the inability in Western church and missionary circles, both Catholic and Protestant, to grapple with the problems of systemic injustice" (432.9). Three nonsystemic approaches to the problems of the poor had been tried in the past couple of centuries and found ineffective. First was the traditional nineteenth-century approach of charity, simply giving people things they did not have. Next in the 1920s was a more comprehensive program including education, health care, and agriculture. From about 1930 onward, "development projects" were the concept in vogue. Development basically meant modernization. None of the three approaches substantially improved the lot of the poor (433.6).

By the 1950s many in the "developing" world had lost confidence in the whole development approach. They were convinced that the poor would never see real improvement until the underlying economic and political structures maintaining their poverty were confronted and drastically changed. "Socio-politically, development was replaced by revolution; ecclesiastically and theologically by *liberation theology*" (434.7).

If "justification by faith" was the phrase that typified the Protestant Reformation, "God's preferential option for the poor" is the phrase that has come to typify liberation theology. It was coined at a meeting of Latin American Roman Catholic bishops in 1979. "The point is ... that the poor are the first, though not the only ones, on which God's attention focuses and that, therefore, the church has no choice but to demonstrate solidarity with the poor" (436.1). "The poor are the marginalized, those who lack every active or even passive participation in society" (436.9), the ones who are routinely passed over by the establishment highways of power, wealth, and status just as slum dwellers are passed over by elevated highways. There are no on-ramps in poor neighborhoods.

If the mission of the church is wrapped up with the lives of the poor, the vocabulary of theology must change. "Salvation," which has a religious and futuristic ring to it, is replaced by "liberation," a concrete change in the here and now. "Fellowship" is replaced by "solidarity." This is no mere playing with words. Imagine the total reorientation of congregational life that would necessarily follow in Western churches if the energy that goes into "fellowship groups" (with other insiders) were diverted to "solidarity groups" (with outsiders, especially poor ones).

Involvement with the poor in mission does not mean doing things *for* them. Mission itself is reconceptualized. The poor are no longer the recipients of mission and charity but the "agents and bearers" of mission (436.4). According to some liberation theologians, they are the ones who will save the world. The poor, once liberated, will help the rich see that they have been blind to their own oppressiveness and to "the idols of money, race, and self-interest" (437.7).

"Liberation" theology, while similar in some ways to the Protestant liberal theology that preceded it (438.3), broke out of the Enlightenment paradigm that liberal theology had assumed. First, liberal theology accepted the Enlightenment's trust in human reason and therefore had to struggle with the question "whether it still makes sense to talk about God in a secular age." The cross dropped completely out of the liberal picture. By contrast, liberation theologians assume that God exists and that the cross is a central image for theology today. God is on the side of the poor; to disregard God's presence and power (as liberal theology tends to do) is to disregard a most important ally in the struggle. That is an utterly ridiculous battle plan for anyone intent on winning (439.1).

Second, liberal theology (like Enlightenment thinking in general) was written from the perspective of the elite. From that angle the political and economic systems that human reason had produced looked like they were generally working. Liberals believed that with a few more adjustments to these systems as suggested by reason in the light of experience, human problems could be solved. By contrast, liberationists produced "theology from below," from the angle of the poor (439.6). From that perspective, the systems did not appear to be working at all. The only hope would be a clean break with the establishment and a new way of doing things.

There is a third sense in which many but not all liberationists have broken with the Enlightenment assumptions. This has to do with "capitalism's twin sister," Marxism (441.3, quoting Newbigin). Like capitalism, Marxism completely accepted the intellectual framework of the Enlightenment. The future of humanity could be engineered by human reason if power were in the hands of reasonable people, which in Marxist terms were the proletariat, the poor.

Some liberationists have been attracted to Marxism's bias for the poor and Marxism's justification of violent overthrow of the established systems. But others, such as José Míguez Bonino, keep a cautious distance from Marxism and point out the historical examples of "its abuse of power, its arbitrariness, its personality cults, and its bureaucratic cliques" (440.7). "The majority [of liberationists] are committed to nonviolence" (442.1). Their goal is reconciliation of the rich and poor, which involves a conversion of both rather than an overpowering of one by the other.

This reflects a maturing in liberation theology over the decades. At first there were many in Latin America who put almost complete trust in political change. But the replacement of right-wing capitalist rulers by socialist regimes did not produce the results that the poor and the liberationists expected. "People were liberated without becoming free" (445.4), which caused the liberationists to take a second, more careful look at their analysis of the situation and the Bible.

One of the leading rethinkers is Juan Luis Segundo. Instead of going to the Bible for a convenient and one-sided political illustration — the national liberation of Israel from slavery in Egypt — Segundo tackles the social theology of Paul. For Paul, human beings are more than political animals, the problems of humanity are partly (largely?) in the human heart rather than in the political structures, Christians should "calculate the energy cost" before starting a fight against a social institution, and Christians can and should transcend their oppression by triumphing over their circumstances, "even where circumstances do not change, even where liberation does not come" (446.5).

This tiny summary may make it appear that Segundo is spiritualizing the struggle and consigning the poor to their fate, but that is not his stance at all. He is digging deep into Paul in order to produce a "spirituality for the long haul" (446.6), a complex reading of the human situation present and future that enables the struggling poor to become resilient. If an apparent "success" in their liberation leads to a setback, if a new leader turns out to be a new oppressor, the Paul-motivated poor do not abandon the struggle because they had never pinned all their hopes on that particular "success" or that particular leader in the first place. They keep on working in light of the ultimate success and the ultimate leader, the Messiah.

Of course, Segundo does not speak for all liberationists and this summary is "not intended to whitewash liberation theology" (447.4). We do, however, need to recognize liberation theology as a new stage in the history of theology and a new strand within the emerging paradigm of mission.

Inculturation

In order to contextualize, any theology must come to grips with the key aspects of a local context. For liberation theology, those key aspects are identified as social class distinctions. For another main form of contextualization called inculturation, the issue is not so much the class distinctions within a culture as the distinction of one culture from others. Liberationists see oppression in political and economic structures within one culture; inculturationists see it as cultural imperialism across cultural lines. Inculturation sets out not so much to free the poor from the oppressors as to free each culture from alien cultural domination.

Though it may sound tame by comparison with the fiery rhetoric of some liberation theologians, inculturation is actually far more radical than the attempts at cultural adjustment of the gospel in previous centuries, which had usually been called "adaptation," "accommodation," or "indigenization" (448.7). Six characteristics distinguish inculturation from those superficial approaches:

1. The agents of the inculturation process are not the professionally trained missionaries but the Holy Spirit and the local converts, especially the laity (453.3).

2. The emphasis is on the local situation in all its aspects — social, economic, political, religious, educational, etc. (453.6).

3. The regional (macrocultural) situation is also in view; for example, the Protestant Reformation can be seen as an inculturation of the faith among Germanic peoples, which was different from its previous (Roman Catholic) inculturation among the Latins of southern Europe (453.7).

4. The incarnation of Christ is the model for inculturation; "It is not so much a case of the church [from one culture] being *expanded,* but of the church being *born anew* in each context and culture" (454.5).

5. Inculturation is more like planting a seed than transplanting a mature tree; one knows that the tree growing from a seed will be of the same species but its exact shape and size cannot be predicted (454.9).

6. Inculturation deals with the local culture as an integrated whole; it does not try to pick off individual features or customs of the culture for inclusion or exclusion (454.9).

On the whole, inculturation rejects the "kernel and husk" view that the Christian faith is a supracultural kernel that remains the same no matter which cultural husk is put around it (449.3). The relationship between the gospel and culture is far more complex than that.

To change images, we could say that any white female missionary in the Congo can put on a fabulous Congolese Sunday dress, but in Kinshasa she will still look like a foreigner trying to fit in. This is similar to *accommodation* as an evangelistic strategy, dressing up the supracultural gospel in local clothing. By contrast, if a white woman grows up as a missionary child socialized in an African village, she can put on the same dress but she will look foreign for only as long as she stands still. When the music starts and she joins in an African worship dance, the secret is out. She moves like an African, and other Africans will say she *is* African. That genuine, inner Africanness is similar to the radical aim of gospel *inculturation.* It allows room for a church to become "self-theologizing" rather than just "self-governing, self-supporting, and self-propagating" (451.9).

Everything we have said so far about inculturation has emphasized making the gospel at home in a culture. This is a healthy corrective to the many mission situations where the church and the gospel have been far too culturally foreign for far too long. However, this corrective introduces a new danger — that the gospel will be made so much at home in local cultures that Christianity becomes "nothing but the religious dimension of the culture — listening to the church, society hears only the sound of its own music" (455.4). This reduction of the church to an uncritical echo of the culture is already the situation in much of the West and may become true in other places as local theologies are legitimized. Wherever it happens, it indicates that the gospel has been co-opted by the culture and lost its gospel-ness, "for that society never existed, in East or West, ancient time or modern, which could absorb the word of Christ painlessly into its system" (455.7, quoting Walls).

Since the church in each culture may get sucked into its own culture unawares, it needs the churches in other cultures to keep talking to it. Outsiders may see glaring weaknesses that insiders overlook. Outsiders may also bring in "previously unknown mysteries of the faith" that were discovered as they inculturated the gospel into unevangelized societies (456.1). Missionaries of the future will have a key role in carrying on this dialogue among the churches of different cultures, which we may call "interculturation," but it will require "a new disposition..., being genuinely teachable" (456.6). This role will continue because cultures always go on changing, which means that within each culture yesterday's inculturation always has to be reworked in order to fit today.

YOUR VIEWS AND YOUR CONTEXT

58. Of a hundred people in your church, how many do you think see the gospel as an announcement of mainly (1) an event, (2) a new theological path of salvation, (3) a new way of worship, (4) a new set of moral standards, (5) a new institution to join? How would your church be different if they all saw it as an event (as Bosch suggests)?

59. Bosch frequently calls for "creative tension" in the new paradigm, such as mission in "bold humility" and "humble boldness." Briefly describe three styles of evangelism: (1) bold but not humble, (2) humble but not bold, (3) both.

60. Choose any of the following definitions of evangelism and explain its significance for your context in the next decade:

    (a) Evangelism is "our opening up of the mystery of God's love to all people" within the larger framework of our total mission."

    (b) "Evangelism is announcing that God, Creator and Lord of the universe, has personally intervened in human history and has done so supremely through the person and ministry of Jesus of Nazareth who is the Lord of history, Savior and Liberator. In this Jesus, incarnate, crucified, and risen, the reign of God has been inaugurated."

    (c) Evangelism is "that dimension and activity of the church's mission which, by word and deed and in the light of particular conditions and a particular context, offers every person and community, everywhere, a valid opportunity to be directly challenged to a radical reorientation of their lives."

61. Bosch says that evangelism cannot aim "at satisfying rather than transforming people." Every Christian must make a personal response of commitment to Christ. What does your theology and your idea of mission do with the millions of people who seem satisfied to belong to a church but do not appear to be transformed by any personal commitment to Christ?

62. How did the Enlightenment produce the blind spot of Western theology among theologians like Schleiermacher and Bultmann? How did the non-Western liberation theologians expose the blind spot in the last few decades?

63. In your own theology of mission, are you more excited about the prospects of contextualization or more concerned about the dangers of overcontextualization? Give an example of one good prospect and one real danger.

64. Andrew Walls wrote that no society could "absorb the word of Christ painlessly into its system." What are two or three of the painful adjustments your society would need to make in order genuinely to take in the good news of God's arriving kingdom?

65. What is "the preferential option for the poor"? How evident is it as a starting point for the theology you have grown up with and the one you are developing in your own thinking?

66. What are some of the ways that the new inculturation Bosch calls for will go deeper than the older "accommodation" did? Give at least one example of the new deeper inculturation in your culture. This may be an example that is already being done or taught or it may be something you think should be introduced.

67. Given your church's history and its current social setting, which kind of mission activity most urgently needs to be increased — evangelization, liberation, or inculturation? What will have to change in order for this increase to happen?

68. Write a prayer inviting God to do whatever needs to be done for your church to be genuinely contextualized in your culture.

D. THE BEARER OF MISSION[7]
The Whole Church in the Whole World
(Bosch, TM, pp. 368–89 and 457–74)[8]

Within the emerging paradigm of mission we have so far looked at *the source, the goals, and the activities of mission.* Mission arises in God himself (the *missio Dei*), sets its sights on salvation and justice, and involves the key activities of evangelism and contextualization. But who carries out these activities? Who does

---

7. Bosch is ambivalent about calling the church the "bearer" of mission. On the one hand, he wants to emphasize that the real "bearer" of mission is God rather than the church: "Neither the church nor any other human agent can ever be considered the author or bearer of mission" (392.8). On the other, he refers to the whole church community rather than the clergy as "the primary bearer of mission" (472.4). Bearer may not be the best word to use, but I was not able to come up with a simple word that would better convey the dual idea of the church both doing the activities of mission and being the embodiment of mission.

8. Bosch's title for this key section of his paradigm is "Mission as the church-with-others." He is following Sundermeier in trying to avoid the paternalistic implications that can be read into Bonhoeffer's famous phrase "the church *for* others" (375.4). But in light of developments in the 1990s after Bosch wrote, "church-with-others" is likely to be misread today as a statement that relativizes Christianity and reduces mission to dialogue-with-others. Though dialogue is by no means out of the picture, Bosch's primary emphasis in his discussion of "church-*for*" and "church-*with*" is on the relation of the Western Church to others Christians and churches, not to other religions (cf. 375.6 and 379.6; on dialogue see 483–89).

the evangelizing and contextualizing in response to the missionary thrust from God and the transformative goals that embody God's concerns? Who has been deputized as the bearer of God's mission?

Obviously it is the church, which is to carry out the will of Christ as a body carries out the will of the head. Whether the *missio Dei* is also carried out through any other religious or social groups will be addressed in our next section on the limits of mission. For now we will focus on the church as the bearer of mission — the whole church in the whole world.

Five things have catastrophically disrupted the unity, integrity, and effectiveness of the church on its mission. All five must be overcome in a new paradigm of mission:

- treating mission as merely one compartment of the church's activity

- treating church and mission as separable concepts

- accepting denominational divisions as inevitable

- treating some churches as "receiving churches" (or younger churches, daughter churches, mission churches, etc.)

- treating the laity as second-class members of the church

1. Compartmentalizing mission (368.7–372.4)

Of the five problems we are considering, compartmentalizing mission has been the dominant one for the past two centuries. In this view, mission is one activity of the church in parallel with other activities such as worship, church administration, and education/formation of church members. Mission activity concerns a very small subset of church members, the missionaries (see Figure 7).

How did we ever come to imagine that the job of carrying the missionary torch was the job of a few specialist professionals and organizations within the church rather than the church as a whole? This happened at the dawn of the modern missionary era in different ways among Catholics and Protestants.

In the Roman Catholic Church (369.3) it came about via *centralization of mission.* In effect mission was delegated from the church as a whole to missionary orders such as the Jesuits. These orders reported directly to the pope. Missionaries were seen as his emissaries, not closely attached to other bishops and dioceses. "Mission" was defined as what these professionals did as adjuncts to the main body of the church.

In most Protestant (pope-less) circles (369.5), the same thing happened by *marginalizing mission.* The denominational leadership of the Protestant churches rarely took any initiative in mission and often opposed those who did. Mission societies came into being as specialist groups on the margins of the established churches. As in the Catholic Church, "mission" was defined largely as

Figure 7
Four Models Relating Church and Mission

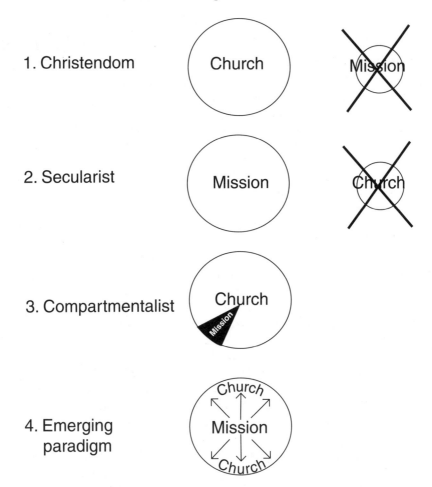

international mission, not part of the everyday life of the ordinary Christian or congregation in the West.

During the twentieth century the compartmentalization broke down. Mission was recognized as a core part of being Christian, not an activity of some Christians. Every aspect of the life of the church is now seen to have a missionary dimension even if it is not specifically missionary in intention (Newbigin; 373.1). Even salvation itself involves not only justification and sanctification but *vocation,* calling to mission (Barth; 373.5). Mission could no more be a compartment of church life than DNA can be a compartment of a human body. It is in every cell, and it identifies each cell as part of one particular body.

The integration of church and mission occurred among Protestants gradually up to the 1960s in steps marked fairly clearly by the series of international missionary meetings (369.7).[9] On the Catholic side, Vatican II (1962–65) marked an abrupt, major shift toward the same view of the whole church as essentially missionary (371.6).

2. Separating church and mission (372.5–378.7)

When church and mission are separated, two results are possible — a missionless church or a churchless mission. Both are impossibilities in theory but realities in history. The missionless church is a church that does not sense God sending it into the world, does not move toward salvation and justice, and does not engage in evangelism and contextualization. It does not conform to the New Testament images of the church — "salt, light, yeast, servant, and prophet" (374.5). Very unfortunately the church in much of Christendom was practically missionless from the fourth to the eighteenth centuries (376.8). Except for the monastic orders (whose impact on the world was considerable), the church as a whole was focused on maintenance of its members and its territory, not on reaching out to any outsiders. It was a living denial that the church is the bearer of mission.

Like the missionless church, the advocates of a churchless mission also deny that the church is the bearer of mission, but for the opposite reason. The churchless mission view, associated especially with Hoekendijk, is that the actual church has become so preoccupied with itself that it is irrelevant for what God is doing in the world. People who want to serve God's purpose of transforming the world today should forget the church and partner with all social groups who are following God's true agenda, whether they acknowledge God himself or not (383.5). Among Hoekendijk's followers it became fashionable to bash the church. The gentler critics said the church itself needed to be redeemed (that is, the church *is* the "mission field"; 384.8). Harsher ones wrote the church off as irredeemable (384.5).

Both Hoekendijk and the missionless church he was attacking failed to see that church and mission are Siamese twins joined at the spine. Detach them and you kill both. Mission is the center of the identity of the church.

An essentially missionary church has to be a church on the move, not a church that has arrived. As *"a sacrament, a sign, and an instrument"* (374.3, my italics), the pilgrim church (373.7) always points beyond itself rather than at itself (376.2). "Its members are not proclaiming, 'Come to us!' but 'Let us follow him!' " (376.6).

The church on the move follows Jesus into the world, not away from it. The negative view of "the world" found in 1 John 2:15 ("Love not the world . . . "), which had long dominated Christian thought, is replaced by the positive view of John 3:16 ("God so loved the world . . . "). The church orients its activity and

---

9. See Appendix A for a classified list of these meetings.

life toward the world (the physical and social world) rather than over against the world (the world of evil and darkness).

3. Resigning to denominational divisions (457.6–464.4)

The modern mission movement among Protestants came out of the Pietist movement, which was the first grassroots experience of transdenominational Christian unity (457.7). Some early mission societies were nondenominational, but the honeymoon period of interdenominational cooperation did not last. By about 1830, mission agencies tended to revert to a denominational identity, which was then exported with the gospel, causing problems that continue to this day. The pendulum swung back toward transdenominationalism in the late nineteenth century with the Student Volunteer Movement and at the landmark Edinburgh mission conference in 1910, then back toward division (between the ecumenical and evangelical blocs rather than between denominations) from about 1920 to 1950. On the mission fields the agencies looked like "a chaotic conglomeration of unrelated, overlapping, often competing units" (458.5, quoting Beaver).

Serious efforts were made to get over denominational barriers by the formation of the International Missionary Council in 1921 (linking mission societies) and the World Council of Churches in 1948 (linking denominations). The two merged in 1961, when it was agreed that their respective agendas of mission and unity belonged together in one organization (459.9). But many evangelicals who had been in the IMC did not go along into the WCC. A new interdenominational movement among evangelicals emerged, flowering especially in the Lausanne conference of 1974.

On the Catholic side, once again we see that Vatican II (1962–65) was a decisive turning point. It marked a huge shift in attitude toward Protestants, who were no longer considered heretics in need of (re)conversion (461.9). Instead they were called "separated brethren," and the need for "the restoration of unity among all Christians" was acknowledged as necessary for the church's credibility in mission (462.7). Protestants and Catholics even began to speak of "common witness" (shared witness, 463.4), a major change from the old habit of throwing rocks at each other.

4. Labeling some churches "receiving churches" (or "daughter churches," 465.9–466.4)

It was to be expected that missionary sending churches with centuries of theological and organizational tradition would see themselves as superior to the fledgling churches they founded, but this paternalistic attitude persisted far longer than it should have. In the mid-twentieth century a number of "marvelous phrases" were coined to point to the new goal of partnership between Western churches and those churches that had resulted from Western-based mission (465.9).

The hollowness of these phrases is best summed up in a comment an Indonesian pastor made about the slogan of the Whitby missionary conference in
1947, "Partnership in obedience." He said to a Dutch professor, "Yes, *partnership* for you but *obedience* for us" (466.1). Things have improved in the last fifty
years, but there is still a long way to go. "We need new relationships, mutual
responsibility, accountability, and interdependence" (466.4).

If the whole church, regardless of geography and ethnicity, is to take the
gospel to the whole world, "the church" must stop being identified primarily
with its power centers in the West. The national and local embodiments of the
church everywhere are now seen as the "real" church, the real agents of mission.
They, rather than professional missionaries and organizations (380.5), are the
missionary face of the church to the world, whether in Rome, New York, Nairobi,
or Beijing.

5. Treating the laity as inferior Christians (467.5–474.5)

"The movement away from ministry as the monopoly of ordained men . . . is
one of the most dramatic shifts taking place in the church today" (467.5). Perhaps
the most controversial aspect of the shift is the ordination of women, but a more
fundamental question is what "ordination," the official dividing line between
clergy and laity, really means, regardless of gender (472.7). That division between
clergy and laity will blur, and it should. The days are over when "the clergyman-
priest, enshrined in a privileged and central position, remained the linchpin of
the church" (470.3).

We must take into account that the church originally did not have a very
religious ring or feel to its identity. Jesus did not choose his disciples from the
priestly class of his day (467.9), the "churches" Paul founded were not called
by a religious label such as "synagogue" or "*thiasoi,* the common Greek term
for . . . religious meetings" (468.3), and Christian clergy were not called "priests"
until about 200 (468.8).

The sharp distinction between laity and clergy, which held for over a millennium, was reinforced in recent centuries by the Enlightenment distinction
between public and private spheres of life (472.9). The clergy were considered
to be specialists in the private sphere, and the laity were to leave that part of
life under their control. As the Enlightenment view breaks down in our time,
Christians recognize that service in the public spheres of life (education, society,
business, politics) is also service to God because God is not restricted to the private sphere (473.3). They also realize that lay people can be much more involved
in preaching, mission, and church leadership than they traditionally have been.
Lay initiatives are mushrooming in Latin America as "base Christian communities," in Africa as "indigenous" or "independent churches," in China and the
West as "house churches." In these cases "the laity have come of age and are
missionally involved in an imaginative way" (473.9). In what may be the single

most decisive shift in the whole emerging paradigm, mission has replaced the clergy at the center of the church's identity.

Conclusion — an imperfect but effective witness

The key to all five of the above problems is the way the church sees its relationship to the world. The challenge today is to find a new perspective that avoids the two traps the evangelical and ecumenical Protestants fell into in the 1960s and 1970s. Evangelicals followed McGavran into the "Church Growth," i.e., church-centered, model of mission, which basically remained within the "old model" in Table 11 (p. 122; 381.9). Ecumenicals followed Hoekendijk into the "churchless mission" model described earlier (383.5). In contrast to both these extremes, let us consider a new model that attempts to hold the two in "creative tension."[10]

Five guidelines are needed as we move from the old to the new model in Table 11. Unfortunately the ecumenical critics of the church in the early 1970s had grasped only the second of these:

1. We must affirm both that the church is a valid entity (called out of the world as a special group) and that it has a valid role (sent into the world to serve, not just to call more people out; 386.1).

2. We must admit that the church is flawed (386.9).

3. We must face the flaws with forgiveness and hope (387.2) for the real church on earth is "an inseparable union of the divine and the dusty" (389.4).

4. We must speak humbly to the world (387.6).

5. We must always look beyond the world while we look at the world, that is, we must not limit ourselves to the world's agenda (387.7).

The creative tension in this view of the church is the familiar one between the "already" and the "not yet" aspects of the arrival of the kingdom of God.[11] "Christianity is not yet the new creation, but it is the working of the Spirit of the new creation" (388.1). That is why the church as we know it is "ambiguous in the extreme" (389.5), at times a true sign of the kingdom and at other times a most misleading body.

The church is a work in progress. Like a lump of clay on a potter's wheel, the church bears the visible imprints of the invisible fingers of God. The world

---

10. Bosch finds this "creative tension" both within biblical authors such as Matthew (81.3) and at key points throughout his own new paradigm, e.g., the tension between dialogue and mission (488.9). The phrase is probably more typical of Bosch's theological style than any other. When his colleagues published a volume of responses to his thought, they titled it *Mission in Creative Tension* (Pretoria: Southern Africa Missiological Society, 1990).

11. See Figure 1 (p. 34), explaining Paul's idea of the "grace period" as a time of overlapping eras.

Table 11
The Relation between the Church and the World (377.7)

	Old model (church in itself)	New model (church in the world)
1. The "world" means . . .	The world of evil	The physical and social world
2. The "church" means . . .	The power centers in the West	All national/local churches
3. Goal of mission	Larger church	Welfare of the world
4. Church and kingdom	Church = kingdom	Church a sign or foretaste
5. Church's focus	Other-worldly	This world and the next
6. Holy Spirit	Our possession	Our possessor and animator
7. Church members	Church people	Kingdom people (378.5)
8. Church's role	Border guard	Herald

cannot see the Potter, but when it sees a lump of clay being worked into the shape of a pot, it knows there must be a Potter around somewhere. The pot, though incomplete, is a sign bearing witness to the Potter's activity and intentions.

The Potter does not create a pot by snapping his fingers but by getting his hands dirty, and that is what the church testifies to — God's willingness to get dirty for the sake of humanity. If the church does not let itself be increasingly molded toward God's creative intentions for the world (which add up to the kingdom), it does not bear its witness to that kind of God. And yet, even by its failures, it creates a new opportunity for the Potter to show his grace and determination. Rather than fling the stubborn lump of clay from his wheel, he continues to work it.

Should we then be difficult in God's hands so he can show off his patience? God forbid! (cf. Rom. 6:1). Rather let us be pliant and, in a thousand places and ways around the world, bear the witness the whole church is supposed to bear, pointing ever more clearly beyond our current state to the future God has in mind. Understanding the history of the various streams of Protestantism (Figure 8), let us see if we can get them to converge again and flow together in a mission marked by the creative tension of the kingdom in the present.

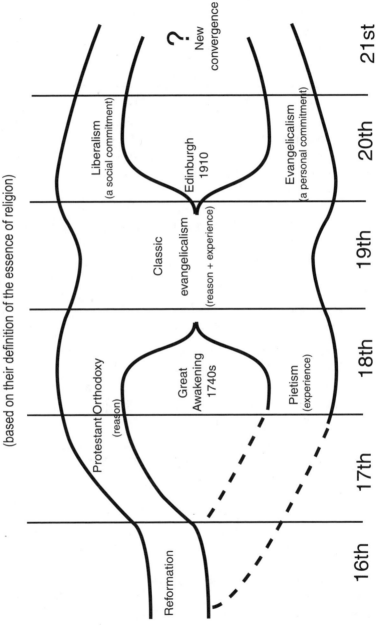

Figure 8
Protestant Streams by Century
(based on their definition of the essence of religion)

YOUR VIEWS AND YOUR CONTEXT

69. To what extent do ordinary church members in your church see that they are (or should all be) participating in the church's work of bearing God's mission? What can be done to help them move beyond the old view of mission as the work of a few professionals?

70. What is the difference between a church that points at itself and a church that points beyond itself? What spoken and unspoken messages is each kind of church sending to the world?

71. Relationships between Catholics and Protestants vary drastically from country to country. How important is it for the two to recognize each other as co-bearers of mission in the new paradigm? What impact would further Catholic-Protestant reconciliation have, if any, on the church's witness in your country?

72. Write a prayer about the relationship of Catholics and Protestants in your country. Ask Jesus to do what needs to be done so that his mission is not hindered by division between his true followers in any church.

73. It has been over half a century since the phrase "partnership in obedience" was coined. What practical strides have been made in genuine partnership? Where are the old patterns of Western assumed superiority and Two-Thirds World "receiving" still visible?

74. Agree or disagree: *The single most decisive shift in the new paradigm is that mission has replaced the clergy at the center of the church's identity.* Explain your reasons.

75. Of the eight contrasts in Table 11 (Church and World, p. 122), choose the two you believe to be the key shifts of perspective your church needs to have about its mission. Explain your choice.

76. What are the strengths and weaknesses of the analogy of the clay and the imperfections of the church God is shaping? Suggest another analogy or picture that conveys your view of the church as the bearer of mission.

E. THE LIMITS OF MISSION
Its "Witness" Nature (Bosch, TM, pp. 474–89)
and Its Time Frame (Bosch, TM, pp. 498–510)

It is an awesome thing for the church to be called by God as a special group within the human race to bear his good news for the benefit of the whole race. It is also a very dangerous thing, as the nation of Israel learned to its sorrow. The danger is that the called group, whether Israel or the church, will become so impressed with its God-given, crucial importance for all humanity that it will overestimate that importance in the total scheme of things.

In our case this temptation takes the form of equating the *missio Dei* with the mission of the church, limiting God to the church as the only means by which he may accomplish his mission for the sake of the world. The way to escape this temptation is to recognize that the church's mission, not God, is the limited thing.

The two limits of the church's mission are obvious and undoubtable — human finitude and historical time. Finitude refers to the finite knowledge and experience of any human being or group. Recognition of finitude humbles the church by putting its mission into an ambiguous relationship with other faiths and ideologies. Time refers to the limited time between the days of Jesus on earth and the yet unknown Day of the Lord, which will end history as we know it. Recognition of this time frame humbles the church by acknowledging Israel's role in the *missio Dei* before the church existed and by leaving the final act of history in the hands of Jesus the King when he returns.

When these two limits are ignored (as they all too often have been in church history), the church as the bearer of mission is crippled with pride and can only limp along on its assignment. On the other hand, when the limits are accepted, the bearer can spring into action and have the tremendous impact God intended in harmony with the parts of the *missio Dei* that operate outside the church. Let us then consider and appreciate the limits God has set.

The knowledge limit — witness among people of other faiths

"The unshaken, massive, and collective certitude of the Middle Ages" (475.6) was that the church is dead right ("infallible") and all other religions are dead wrong ("outside the church there is no salvation," or in the later Protestant view, "outside the Word there is no salvation"; 475.1). For Catholics and Protestants alike, "mission essentially meant *conquest* and *displacement*" of any other faith (475.1).

The Enlightenment rejected this view of Christian mission completely. It held three things to be true of all religions: (1) their value was relative and had to be debated on the basis of reason, (2) their "truth" applied only to the world of value, not the world of facts, and (3) humanity would lose interest in all the religions as people gradually and inevitably came to base their lives more on facts alone (475.7). The third point was most ardently believed in the 1960s and has been in hasty retreat ever since, as religions and spirituality of all types have made a startling comeback (476.3).

The first two points, however, are still widely believed. Their challenge to the church today has been intensified by massive twentieth-century migrations of people of other faiths into traditionally Christian regions. These two challenges — the Enlightenment's claim that Christian mission is *unnecessary* (because reason is a surer guide to life than theology is) and the claim of other religions that Christian mission is *imperialistic* (if it does not accept them as equals when they move in next door) — are today "the two largest unsolved problems for the Christian church" (476.9).

To say they are unsolved does not mean they are unaddressed. Already in 1970, Nurnberger listed twenty-seven varieties of theologies of religions (478.4)! Even today there is no consensus emerging among all these theories, which can be roughly grouped into three types, as shown in Table 12.

The problem with all three types of theories — exclusivism (478.7), fulfillment (479.4), relativism (481.5) — is that "they are all too neat" (483.4), especially the first one with its "comfortable claim to absoluteness" and the last with its "arbitrary pluralism" (483.3, 486.7). They explain everything, that is, they purport to fathom the mystery of the relation of Christianity to other faiths and force it to make logical sense.

The inadequacy of that approach, especially in the case of pluralism, can be shown by a diagram parallel to the three others in previous sections — Bosch's emerging paradigm, the evangelical and liberationist paradigms. The pluralist diagram (see Figure 9) makes everything appear very simple. God (or "good") aims at love and goodness. The different religions, cultures, and historical

Table 12
Three Approaches to a Theology of Religions

	Pre-modern examples	Modern examples	Post-modern examples[1]
1. **"Exclusivism"** (only Christianity is right)	Traditional Catholic Traditional Protestant	Current evangelicals	Barth
2. **"Fulfillment"**[2] (Christianity fulfills the good to be found partially in others)	Xavier, de Nobili, Ricci (early Jesuits in Asia)	Farquhar Hocking Vatican II	Rahner ("anonymous Christians")
3. **"Relativism"**[3] (all religions are valued)		Troeltsch	Knitter Pannikar

[1] Some of the writers in this column pre-date post-modernism. To say they are "post-modern examples" means that their style of thinking about theology of religion has some elements which today would be called post-modern.

[2] Similar to the category now more commonly labeled "inclusivism."

[3] "Pluralism" is the more common term now.

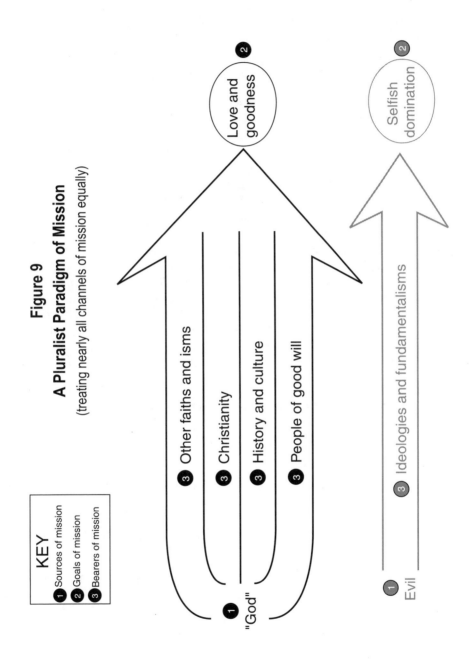

Figure 9
A Pluralist Paradigm of Mission
(treating nearly all channels of mission equally)

KEY
1 Sources of mission
2 Goals of mission
3 Bearers of mission

Love and goodness — 2

Selfish domination — 2

3 Other faiths and isms
3 Christianity
3 History and culture
3 People of good will

3 Ideologies and fundamentalisms

1 "God"

1 Evil

processes are parallel paths from God to love. They should all recognize each other as equal partners in "God's" mission. There is a second, smaller reality at the bottom of the diagram that pluralists believe in but prefer not to discuss because it complicates things. The groups at the bottom do not fit in. They are the groups that claim three things that are intolerable to pluralists: (1) they are right, (2) other groups are wrong, and (3) if only they could get enough power, they would prove the first two points to everyone. Pluralists exclude them from God's mission dogmatically and absolutely.

A sounder approach than any of the three in Table 12 (p. 126) would admit the limits of our knowledge by keeping some creative tension among all three views and acknowledging that understanding other faiths and ideologies is as much a matter of the heart as of the mind (483.7). This is not to back away from giving our witness. Quite the contrary. "Dialogue means witnessing to our deepest convictions, whilst listening to those of our neighbors" (484.4). "The Christian faith cannot surrender the conviction that God, in sending Jesus Christ into our midst, has taken a definitive and eschatological course of action and is extending to human beings forgiveness, justification, and a new life of joy and servanthood, which, in turn, calls for a human response in the form of conversion" (488.2). As the San Antonio meeting of the WCC put it, "We affirm that witness does not preclude dialogue but invites it, and that dialogue does not preclude witness but extends and deepens it" (487.2).

To abandon this witness would dissolve the creative tension we are talking about and forfeit the creativity. We want to retain the tension and the accompanying creativity for as long as we are bound by the limits of human knowledge. Therefore we adopt the following attitudes and approaches:

1. "Accepting the coexistence of different faiths and to do so not grudgingly but willingly" (483.7).

2. Expecting in dialogue with people of other faiths to meet the God who has been working in them before our arrival (484.6).

3. Relating differently to each other faith depending on its own nature (not having one standard approach to all other faiths simply because they are not Christian (485.7).

4. Recognizing that faiths are not merely or primarily techniques to gain salvation after death (488.5).

5. Admitting "we do not have all the answers . . . , anticipating surprises as the Spirit guides us into fuller understanding" (489.3).

Most exclusivists reject all five of these points because they appear relativistic. We need to say a bit more about the last two points, which crucially distinguish this position from relativism.

On the fourth point, we note that relativists and exclusivists tend to agree that religions are primarily salvation systems and then to debate whether salvation is found in all systems or only in the Christian one. But their shared view of religion as primarily a means of salvation after death is not a truly Christian view. "Conversion [to Christianity] is . . . not the joining of a community in order to procure 'eternal salvation'; it is, rather, a change in allegiance in which Christ is accepted as Lord and center of one's life. A Christian is not simply somebody who stands a better chance of being 'saved,' but a person who accepts the responsibility to serve God in this life and promote God's reign in all its forms" (488.7). The Christian convert is not focused on salvation but on Jesus Christ the Lord. Salvation after death comes to the Christian a bit like an inheritance comes to a widow from her husband — it is certain (if she outlives him) but it was never supposed to be the main reason she married him in the first place.

As for the fifth point, our openness to new understanding is "not opting for agnosticism, but for humility. It is, however, a bold humility or a humble boldness. We know only in part, but we do know. And we believe that the faith we profess is both true and just, and should be proclaimed. We do this, however, *not as judges or lawyers, but as witnesses;* not as soldiers, but as envoys of peace; not as high-pressure salespersons, but as ambassadors of the Servant Lord" (489.4, my italics). We recognize that the enemy of God's mission is attempting to obstruct and pervert all aspects of that mission, including especially the church since it is the prime carrier of the mission (see Figure 10, p. 130).

The time limits — between Pentecost and parousia

In addition to the limits of human knowledge, we must understand that Christian mission is bounded by two historical dates — the Day of Pentecost at the beginning and the Day of the return of Christ at the end. All Christian mission is done while keeping one eye on that past Day and the other on that future Day. These two historical reference points guarantee that the Christian missionary anywhere, at any time, in any situation will be able to operate with both confidence and hope and that Christian mission will always be intertwined with the history of the whole world, not isolated in a religious or mystical compartment.

This framework in historical time provided power, urgency, and integrity for the church on its mission throughout the New Testament era. Tragically for mission, this framework was lost in the second, third, and fourth centuries as the church grew in the Greek world and came increasingly under Greek cultural influence. Greek philosophers viewed time as a continuing circle rather than a line (500.4). In its Greek (Hellenized) adaptation, the gospel was no longer seen as an announcement of what time it was (wake-up time!) but a set of timeless truths adding up to a universal religion. The church's theological energy went not into discussion of Pentecost, the return of Christ, or mission in the meantime but rather to the beginning of time — the "origin" of Christ and the relation of the persons in the Trinity (500.6).

The "timeless" approach developed in three forms that together dominated the church until the late nineteenth century. The Greek form emphasized the

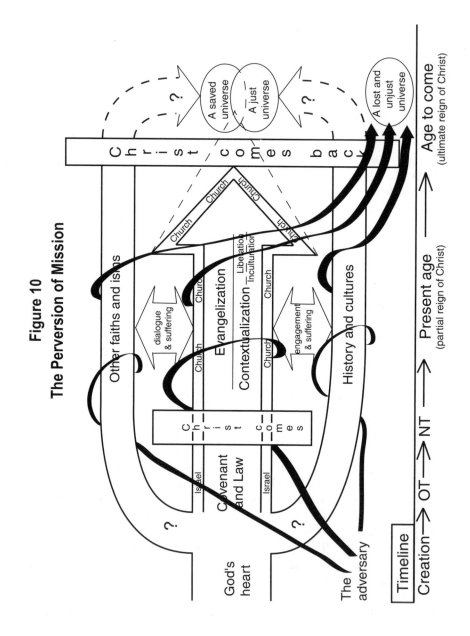

Figure 10
The Perversion of Mission

gradual *theosis* of individuals and the church, that is, their transformation into ever clearer images of God (500.7). The Catholic form emphasized the church as the fulfillment of Jesus' prediction about the coming reign of God (the church *is* the future kingdom made visible today). Many Protestants took a mystical view of the return of Christ, somewhat similar to the Greek view. All three still gave lip service to the return of Christ as a coming historical event, but the prospect of it did not fire them up for their mission.

The Puritans of the seventeenth and eighteenth centuries were a notable exception to this. Because they believed God had a plan for the entire world (not just for individual Christians or the church) and that he was working the plan out in historical phases, "authors like Jonathan Edwards and Samuel Hopkins fanned missionary enthusiasm and stimulated the dispersion of North American missionaries across the globe" (501.3). However, in the nineteenth century the connection between mission and eschatology faded into the background again. Mission was not seen as an activity for a critical moment/era in history but rather as a natural, organic growth that would continue for as long as it needed to reach maturity (501.8).

The rediscovery of the importance of the Day of the Lord[12] came from German and Swiss theologians rather than missionaries, but it was to have huge implications for mission. Several schools of thought developed (502.3):

- Dialectical eschatology, the younger Barth (502.5)
- Existential eschatology, Bultmann (502.7)
- Actualized eschatology, Althaus (503.1)
- Salvation-historical eschatology, Cullmann (503.6).

The fourth approach, which became by far the most influential among mission thinkers, related eschatology to the reign of God in this world. "The new age [of God's reign] has begun; the old has not yet ended. We live between the times, between Christ's first and his second coming; this is the time of the Spirit, which means that it is the time for mission" (503.6). The future reign is already arriving among us (see Figure 11, p. 132).

We still must beware of two opposite dangers. "We may become guilty of the sin of temerity, confusing God's reign with what we have achieved in this world; we may, however, also become guilty of the sin of timidity, hoping for less than has been promised. This world may indeed be enemy-occupied territory, but the enemy has no property rights in it.... He is a usurper" (506.6). Therefore we should write off neither the church, as do those optimists who identify salvation

---

12. Bosch does not note that the rediscovery of the importance of the Day of Pentecost happened at about the same time as the rediscovery of eschatology. It was an experiential rather than a theological discovery, yet the resulting Pentecostal movement was perhaps *the* decisive shift in mission in the twentieth century. Perhaps Bosch passes it by because the movement has remained largely in the sphere of the practice of mission rather than the theology of mission, which is his primary concern. A historical and missiological treatment of perceptions of the importance of Pentecost would make a potent parallel to Bosch's treatment of eschatology. Who will write it?

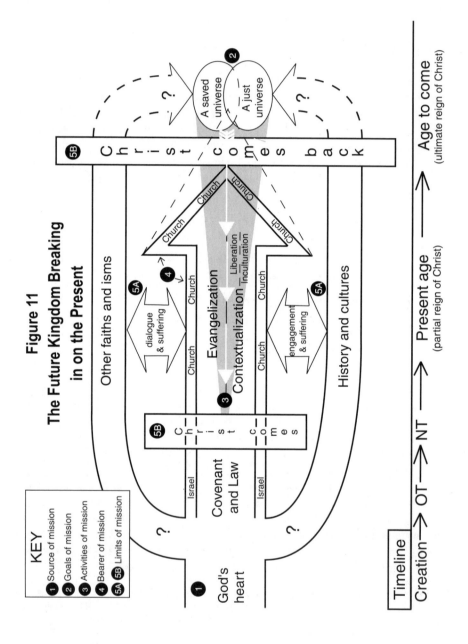

Figure 11
The Future Kingdom Breaking in on the Present

history with secular history (506.8), nor the world, as do those pessimists who completely separate salvation history from secular history (505.7).

"We need an eschatology for mission which is both future-directed and oriented to the here and now. It must be an eschatology that holds in creative and redemptive tension the already and the not yet; the world of sin and rebellion, and the world God loves; the new age that has already begun and the old that has not yet ended. . . . Since God's victory is certain, believers can work both patiently and enthusiastically, blending careful planning with urgent obedience, motivated by the patient impatience of the Christian hope" (508.4).

Patient impatience? Yes. Both are true because we are "living in the force-field [kingdom] of the assurance of salvation already received and the final victory already secured" (509.1). While accepting the limits of our own knowledge, we proclaim our unlimited Lord. While accepting the limits of the age of our mission (510.4), we proclaim the one who will bring in the next age. We cannot do less than he has commissioned us to do; we dare not try to do more.

YOUR VIEWS AND YOUR CONTEXT

77. People may expect a model of mission to include the source, goal, activities, and bearer but they may be surprised to see "limits of mission" as one of the basic categories in a model. How does this surprising component strengthen (or weaken) the paradigm as a whole?

78. Bosch says the two biggest challenges for mission today are the Enlightenment's claim that mission is unnecessary and the claim of other religions that mission is imperialistic. If these are the two biggest, what would you say is the next biggest one and why?

79. Agree or disagree: *The question whether or how God saves people who belong to other religions is much discussed but is not really the key question in a theology of religions because one does not need to answer that question before going ahead and engaging in Christian witness.* Explain your reasons.

80. If possible, give an example or two of surprises from the Spirit that foreign missionaries have run into as they went about their mission in your country or that missionaries from your country found in their service overseas.

81. How much influence does the prospect of Christ's return have on the faith and life of ordinary members of your church? How conscious are they of "living in the force-field of . . . a final victory already secured"?

82. Nowhere in his book does Bosch have more "creative tensions" than in these areas of the limits of mission. To what extent do you see his tensions as the best possible "solutions" to these complex issues? To what extent are they fancy ways of saying there is no solution?

83. Write a one-paragraph prayer that expands the classic eschatological prayer of the Bible, "Come, Lord Jesus" (Rev. 22:20).

F. THE STUDY OF MISSION
Missiology and Theology
(Bosch, TM, pp. 489–98)

We have now considered the source, the goals, the activities, the bearer, and the limits of Christian mission. We need to take one more step back and reflect on the process of considering or studying such things. Today that process is called missiology, but it was not always so. The history of the relationship between mission and theology will show us how we got to where we are today and suggest where missiology and theology should go from here.

As we noted at the beginning, mission was originally the "mother of theology" (489.7), that is, Christians like Paul started to think and write theology because of the questions that arose as they evangelized and planted churches in various cultures. After Christianity became the official religion of the Roman Empire, theology turned philosophical and has largely remained so to the present day (495.8).

At the time of the Enlightenment, theology as a scholarly discipline was divided into theory (biblical studies, systematic theology, church history) and practice (practical theology, i.e., serving the church by preaching, administering sacraments, etc.; 490.1).

When the modern missionary movement emerged and the study of mission was called for, it was at first treated as a subtopic of practical theology. Gradually through the efforts of missiologists like Gustav Warneck and Josef Schmidlin, missiology came to be recognized as a new theological discipline distinct from the other four listed above (491.3).

This recognition was a "mixed blessing" (491.9). "Missiology became the theological institution's 'department of foreign affairs,' dealing with the exotic but at the same time peripheral.... Other teachers regarded themselves as being absolved of any responsibility to reflect on the missionary nature of theology" (492.2). Missiologists were often regarded by other theologians as merely cheerleaders for mission or recruiters for the mission agencies (497.8).

This will not do for the coming era or even for today. Theologians are long overdue to recognize that "theology, rightly understood, has no reason to exist other than critically to accompany the *missio Dei*. So mission should be 'the theme of all theology' " (494.5, quoting Gensichen). "For theology it is a matter of life and death that it should be in direct contact with mission and the missionary enterprise" (494.6). Since so many theologians are still out of touch with mission, "missiology acts as a gadfly in the house of theology" (496.8).

For example, why are systematic theologians today thoroughly trained in philosophy but not in the social sciences? Why do theologians leave the study of other religions to specialists in those fields rather than engaging the questions those religions raise? Why do Western theologians see no problems in being monocultural thinkers? (495.9).

Similarly missiology may ask the church historians why they have paid so much attention to the histories and the distinctives of various denominations and so little to some massive missiological issues in church history, such as (495.5):

- How the Jews were lost in the Greek church
- How the large church in North Africa practically vanished under Islam
- How the church participated in colonial exploitation
- How the official "church" in Europe came to be identified with the elite.

Besides its role in challenging other theological disciplines, missiology has a role in examining, strengthening, and purifying the practice of mission (496.9). As it looks at the relationship between God, the world, and the church, missiology constantly moves back and forth between the biblical text and the current context. This is always a delicate dance. Traditionally the common mistake was to look only at the text and pay too little attention to the current context. Today the main temptation is just the opposite. Both temptations must be avoided if missiology is to address its main challenge, "to link the always-relevant Jesus event of twenty centuries ago to the future of the promised reign of God for the sake of meaningful initiatives in the present" (498.6, quoting van Engelen).

YOUR VIEWS AND YOUR CONTEXT

84. What would be a proper "gadfly" role for mission scholars in your institution? What evidence do you see that a mission perspective is already present in the minds of the people who teach biblical studies, systematic theology, and church history? What evidence is there that they see mission as a specialist subject taught by someone else?

85. How does the study of mission improve the practice of mission? Give an example of an insight from Bosch's book on the theology of mission that could improve the way your church and/or missionaries you know put mission into practice.

86. Write a prayer inviting God to change anything he has to change in order for your church to become a mission-centered church, perfectly aligned with the *missio Dei*.

Chapter 13

Mission in Many Modes

(Bosch, TM, pp. 511–19)

The title *Transforming Mission* "means both that mission is to be understood as an activity that transforms reality and that there is a constant need for mission itself to be transformed" (511.6). The most fundamental thing under continuing transformation is the definition of mission itself.

The Willingen Conference (1952) provided a definition that has served as a benchmark for half a century: our mission is summed up in the word "witness," and "this *witness* is given by *proclamation, fellowship* and *service*" (512.1). We need to stretch even that definition further today. "In attempting to do this we may perhaps move close to viewing everything as mission, but this is a risk we will have to take. Mission is a multifaceted ministry, in respect of witness, service, justice, healing, reconciliation, liberation, peace, evangelism, fellowship, church planting, contextualization, and much more" (512.3).

Analysis will never capture it. We get closer if we pick up on six events in the mission of Jesus himself, since he is the model missionary as well as the author and finisher of our mission. Each of the six has often been emphasized by particular blocs of Christians, as shown in Table 13. We need to find a way to weave them all together.

1. **The incarnation**: "The Western church has been tempted to read the gospels — in Kahler's famous phrase — as 'passion histories with extensive introductions' " (513.4). We do not really get down to serious theology until we reach the cross. The human side of Jesus the God-man, including his ability to identify with the suffering and marginalized social groups in his own day, does not strike us as very important. Liberationists are renewing the church's appreciation for this aspect of Jesus' life and emphasizing it as a central part of the good news.

2. **The cross**: The cross, "the badge of distinction of the Christian faith" (513.9), has always been central to Catholic and Protestant mission. It is a sacrificial model for our mission, a symbol of reconciliation and of forgiveness, especially forgiveness of enemies. "Among the moral teachers of

Table 13
Aspects of Christology

Event	Group emphasizing it	Missiological implications
1. Incarnation	Orth., R.C., Anglican, liberationist	Jesus as a flesh-and-blood human who can identify with others in their suffering
2. Cross	R.C., Protestant	Humble suffering; reconciliation; forgiveness of enemies
3. Resurrection	Orthodox	The center of the missionary message and the call for us to show this new life
4. Ascension	Calvinist, ecumenical	The reign of God in heaven and on earth; the slain lamb as the one on the throne
5. Pentecost	Charismatic	The era of the Spirit; God's power and presence among us now
6. Parousia	Adventist	The coming reign of God as a focus and a magnet affecting us already

the world Christ alone does not make everything depend on moral success" (514.8). And yet in its magnificent complexity, the cross does not represent mere moral tolerance or a natural and understandable example of love. It is a horrific price paid by shocking love. "And if, in the postmodern era, it may seem as if religion is once again acceptable and natural — as Capra and others argue — it has to be pointed out that a religion of the cross cannot be natural; the cross constitutes a permanent danger to any religiosity" (514.1).

3. **The resurrection**: "The most common summary of the early church's missionary message was that it was witnessing to the resurrection of Christ. It was a message of joy, hope, and victory, the first fruit of God's ultimate triumph over the enemy. And in this joy and victory believers may already share" (515.4). The Eastern church has retained this emphasis. So should we all, not merely by announcing it but by living the life right now as signs

that God's life is arriving. By living that life, we announce the imminent death of death and everything that deadens. We "unmask modern idols and false absolutes" (515.7).

4. **The ascension**: The ascension was particularly important in Calvin's theology with its strong emphasis on the sovereignty or reign of Christ. Christ's ascension was ascension to the throne from which he, the sacrificed lamb, now reigns over heaven and earth. "The principle of self-sacrificing love is ... enthroned at the very centre of the reality of the universe" (516.6, quoting WCC Melbourne conference statement). Since Christ's reign is over the world and not just over the church, "it should be natural for Christians to be committed to justice and peace in the social realm" (516.2).

5. **Pentecost**: The Pentecostal and charismatic movements in the twentieth century have brought this event to the fore in mission thinking and practice. If the Spirit of Jesus is on the loose among us, anything is possible. The quest for God's material blessings and repeated experiences of his presence here and now has not always been balanced with an emphasis on (1) the everyday life of the community that the Spirit created (517.1), (2) the boldness the Spirit gives that community as it encounters opposition to its witness (516.9), and (3) the commitment of that community to the wider human community which the Spirit also loves (517.2).

6. **The parousia**: Church history is checkered with adventist, "end-of-the-world" groups who gave up all hope for the present world and focused on the imminent return of Christ, sometimes predicting the year or even the day. For them mission meant calling others to drop out of normal history and join them in waiting for the dawn of superhistory with the arrival of Christ. But belief in a literal return of Christ need not take this either-or form. "In an authentic eschatology the vision of God's ultimate reign of justice and peace serves as a powerful magnet — not because the present is empty, but precisely because God's future has already invaded it" (517.7; see also Figure 11 on p. 132). Instead of undermining the church's present involvement in this world, the prospect of Christ's ultimate takeover propels the church out into the world as a sign of things to come.

Each of the above six events is so dazzling and overwhelming by itself that it is no wonder different churches have become preoccupied with just one or two of them. If we really are supposed to build our mission around all six at once, "who, which church, which human body of people, is equal to such a calling?" (518.5). None of us will qualify. Looking back over church history from the first twelve disciples onward, a person could reasonably ask, "If God has a mission to accomplish, couldn't he find any better representatives than this?" (519.2). It seems that all his ambassadors have sinned and come short of the mission of God (cf. Rom. 3:23).

Nevertheless, we do not despair. We are not on a mission because we qualified for it but because we are being qualified for it. The mission started before we did, and it was not by our choice. "It is not the church which 'undertakes' mission; it is the *missio Dei* which constitutes the church" (519.6).

"Looked at from this perspective mission is, quite simply, the participation of Christians in the liberating mission of Jesus..., wagering on a future that verifiable experience seems to belie. It is the good news of God's love, incarnated in the witness of a community, for the sake of the world" (519.9).

YOUR VIEWS AND YOUR CONTEXT

87. Bosch says mission includes "witness, service, justice, healing, reconciliation, liberation, peace, evangelism, fellowship, church planting, contextualization, and much more." If you think this definition is too broad, narrow it. If you think it is good, defend its breadth.

88. Rank the six aspects of Christology in Bosch's new paradigm in order of how prominent each one is in your church's definition of mission. The six are: incarnation, cross, resurrection, ascension, Pentecost, and parousia. How happy do you think Bosch would be with the way your church prioritizes these? Why?

89. Since the cross has been so central to Catholic and Protestant versions of the gospel, how do we explain the fact that the resurrection, not the cross, is the central theme of all the sermons and speeches in the book of Acts? Acts describes the church in its mission more fully than any other New Testament book. How can the cross be mentioned so little if genuine evangelism is going on?

90. It seems that some churches are more excited about Pentecost than about Jesus' death and resurrection while others preach the gospel without even mentioning Pentecost. What do you consider to be the right amount of emphasis on it compared to the other five Christological themes Bosch mentions?

91. Bosch's closing definition of mission is: "the participation of Christians in the liberating mission of Jesus..., wagering on a future that verifiable experience seems to belie. It is the good news of God's love, incarnated in the witness of a community, for the sake of the world." Explain this definition in your own words as you would explain it to people who have never studied theology. Emphasize the parts of the definition you think are most important for all believers to grasp in order to catch the fire of doing God's mission.

Chapter 14

Responses to Bosch

Bosch's *Transforming Mission* has become the most widely used mission text-book in the world. The complete text is available in French, Spanish, Portuguese, Russian, Chinese, Japanese, Korean, and Indonesian. It is very frequently quoted in a huge variety of writings.

It is not possible here to interact with all the reviews, discussions, articles, and conferences that have considered Bosch's work in the past decade. In fact, even to catalogue them would be a task far beyond the scope and budget for this book. Our much more modest approach will include only two parts: (a) an overview of the thirteen essays published in 1996 as *Mission in Bold Humility: David Bosch's Work Considered,*[1] and a few personal reflections of my own on mission trends since those essays were published.

A. MISSION IN BOLD HUMILITY

Types of content

The thirteen articles in *Mission in Bold Humility* may be grouped as follows:

Biographical material

- Chapter 1. *Saayman and Kritzinger,* Bosch's character, context, and influence as observed by two of his closest colleagues

- Chapter 2. *Verstraelen,* Bosch's life and thought in the context of Africa as a whole

- Chapter 13. *Castro,* Bosch's ecumenical orientation and involvement

Critiques of the book as a whole

- Chapter 2. *Verstraelen,* includes many of Bosch's other writings and reflects on his missiology as a whole

---

1. Willem Saayman and Klippies Kritzinger, eds., *Mission in Bold Humility: David Bosch's Work Considered* (Maryknoll, N.Y.: Orbis Books, 1996). The title is a quote from a key paragraph in Bosch (489.5).

- Chapter 3. *Saayman,* the closest thing to a "review" of the whole book

- Chapter 11. *Sugden,* similar to Saayman in scope but coming from a British evangelical

Comments and critiques on particular topics

- Chapter 5. *Cadorette,* Bosch's description and interpretation of liberation theology in Latin America

- Chapter 6. *Kavunkal,* Bosch's eschatology in relation to contextualization and other religions (Indian context)

- Chapter 9. *Anderson,* Bosch's theology of religions (American context)

Expanding or supplementing Bosch

- Chapter 4. *Pobee,* Bosch opening the way for a genuinely African theology

- Chapter 7. *Shenk,* Bosch's call for theology everywhere to become mission-centered

- Chapter 8. *Robert,* a historical description of the role of American and South African women in shaping the mission vision of South African Christians

- Chapter 10. *Burrows,* "Catholic radical inculturation" as a possible seventh paradigm in addition to Bosch's six

- Chapter 12. *Guider,* suggestions on how missionaries themselves may cope with the massive new demands put on them by the complex factors in Bosch's emerging paradigm

Major contributions of Bosch acknowledged

In the following pages (141–45), all page references refer to *Mission in Bold Humility,* not to *Transforming Mission.*

1. Paradigm perspective

So much academic writing is microscopic that our sense of the meaning and direction of the whole is often lost in the details. When a panoramic writer like Bosch comes along, it is a breath of fresh air. Because of the wide range of his reading and thinking, Bosch was able to step back far enough from New Testament studies, theology, church history, and missiology to articulate and compare the paradigm shifts that affected them all from era to era. By raising our awareness of the Enlightenment paradigm that has dominated the modern mission era, he enables us to critique it and move beyond it without throwing away the valuable aspects of it. These contributions are appreciated, almost taken for granted, by several of the writers in *Mission in Bold Humility.*

2. Excellent capsule summaries of a wide range of missiological issues

One often finds that sections of *Transforming Mission* can stand on their own almost as potted answers to a particular missiological question or summaries of the (then) current debate on a given issue such as evangelism or contextualization. Bosch's treatment of Scripture frequently gives very fresh perspectives on well-worn texts. His historical treatments are generally perceptive (though much more so on the Protestant side than the Catholic and Orthodox). His combination of substance and style makes him highly quotable.

3. Provocative starting point for discussion and development

Burrows says, "Viewing the tremendous success of *Transforming Mission,* I have grown concerned lest it be treated as the *end* of conversation about Christian vocation rather than as an aid to orient ourselves for voyages into uncharted territories" (121.6). Readers ought not to take Bosch to be giving the final word on an issue, because his intention was only to provide an opening background statement, expecting discussion and debate to follow.

Guider warns of the danger at the other extreme. Bosch is so good at raising issues and challenges that the reader may easily be overwhelmed by it all. Far from feeling that all the pieces of the missiological puzzle have now been put into place and all issues resolved, the reader gets from Bosch a better idea of how much is unresolved, and it is staggering (see Guider's six-point summary on 158.3).

Several of the contributors to *Mission in Bold Humility* pick up on one of Bosch's starting points and run with it. Pobee credits Bosch not with providing an African missiology but laying the foundations for one by his critique of Western missiology and his emphasis on the true nature and calling of the church, "being the sign and vehicle of the hope which is denied those who are marginalized and oppressed and dehumanized" (56.9). Pobee then suggests some lines for an African theology, centering on Ela's concept of a "Passover from the language of death to the language of life" (58.7).

Shenk picks up on Bosch's eloquent plea for the entire academic discipline of theology to recover its missionary focus. Theology for too long has been the study of God sitting still. We need a dynamic, missiological theology, the study of God on the move. Shenk spells out a framework for such a theology, which starts not with the doctrine of God but with the doctrine of the reign of God, that is, God on a mission. "The *missio Dei* is essential to the integrity of theology" (84.2).

Cadorette, Kavunkal, and Anderson, like Pobee and Shenk, build on a partic-ular issue that Bosch has identified, but do so more critically. Cadorette's work is described below in criticism 3 ("outdated descriptions," p. 145). Kavunkal applies Bosch's views on interreligious dialogue to the Indian context, appreciat-ing the "creative tension" Bosch has between eschatology and mission. He goes much further than Bosch in a pluralist direction, calling for "enreligionization" rather than mere "inculturation" (74.2), centering Jesus' mission on the idea of love, and identifying the core of Christianity as the "God-experience of Jesus Christ as the 'Abba' " (76.7).

Anderson also tackles the issue of theology of religions. He summarizes recent North American discussions of this topic and briefly describes Bosch's contribution. He notes that *Transforming Mission* inexplicably omits something that was prominent in the study guide on the theology of religions that Bosch wrote for his university, namely "the categories of *continuity* and *discontinuity* in the relationship between God's revealing and redeeming activity in Christ and his activity among people of other faiths" (120.7).

4. Personal integrity and sacrificial commitment to church unity and mission

"David tried to live as one who knew that the value of a theologian's life will be judged not in terms of intellectual rigor and academic originality, but in terms of what the least of Jesus' sisters and brothers experienced in their contact with that scholar" (4.4). He had the personal integrity that was so conspicuously lacking in the whole apartheid power structure. Saayman and Kritzinger, two of his closest colleagues, summarize his trademarks:

- a consistent and disarming honesty
- a deep empathy with people who suffer
- a refusal to impose suffering on others
- a "catholic" commitment to defuse tension and facilitate reconciliation between different Christians and groups (7.4)

Castro concludes, "David J. Bosch was an ecumenist who had the courage to remain in his [Dutch Reformed, South African] tradition while not retaining the divisive elements of his ecclesial and national background" (166.8).

Major criticisms made of Bosch's approach and work

1. Too Western (and male) in sources and intellectual approach[2]

Bosch argues strongly for the importance of contextualization in mission, but he is criticized for not being contextual enough in his own sources and method. Verstraelen and Sugden make the strongest statements on this point.

Verstraelen notes that among the over four hundred authors cited in *Transforming Mission,* only "seven [are] from Asia, ten from Africa, and eleven from Latin America. On closer inspection, one discovers that these theologians are referred to marginally — with the exception of Gutiérrez and Segundo" (13.9).

---

2. This criticism was a major factor which led Norman Thomas (not a contributor to *Mission in Bold Humility*) to compile a volume of works by women and Two-Thirds World writers. See Norman Thomas, *Classic Texts in Mission and World Christianity* (Maryknoll, N.Y.: Orbis Books, 1995), xv.

Bosch's own theological method is one of "developing ideas.... [It] applies theological doctrine to particular situations. This is not, one readily sees, a liberation theology method" (13.5).[3]

Sugden asks, "Is Bosch's approach a history of ideas approach, or does he adequately describe and evaluate the institutions which expressed and promoted these paradigms?" He implies that Bosch's new paradigm is useful but needs to be supplemented with a more direct critique of the three institutions (capitalism, the bureaucratic state, and universities and media) that embody the modern paradigm (140.8).

Sugden identifies another weak point in Bosch's use of sources. "Many concerns Bosch records [such as 'interculturation'] have been raised for a number of years by Two-Thirds World Evangelicals. But they are not credited with them" (149.1). Instead the ideas of people in this group show up in Bosch only when they have been quoted by Western missionaries or scholars.

Saayman, while he does not strongly criticize the intellectual approach of *Transforming Mission,* argues that the essential work of contextualization remains for others to do. "If an important and magisterial book such as this is to become really useful, it needs specifically contextual responses from theologians in general and missiologists in particular, especially from those in the Third World" (40.7). Saayman's major concern is that Bosch is overly cautious about the danger of "contextualism" (contextualization in which the local culture is given decisive authority over the biblical text). Saayman believes that in the South African context, theologians still have a long way to go before they need to worry about this (50–51).

2. Some large gaps, especially on the significance of Pentecostal mission

Saayman notes Bosch's "near total silence about the Pentecostal contribution to mission" (51.7). This he describes as "strange" and "hardly justifiable" in light of the size and strength of the movement (see below, p. 146). Bosch does allow a larger place in his theology of mission for the Holy Spirit than many of his fellow theologians in the Reformed tradition do; however, his proposed framework for a new paradigm of mission focuses much more on Christ than on the Holy Spirit, as is clear in his final chapter (511f.).

Another omission noted by Saayman (51.9) is that of the contribution of women to mission and the place of womanist theology as an example of liberation theology. This relates to the first criticism above, that Bosch's sources were overwhelmingly male.

Burrows points out that Bosch "seems to have missed" the "Catholic Inculturation Paradigm" that was developed by Jesuits in Asia centuries ago, then

---

3. Verstraelen notes and illustrates that Bosch is more contextual in much of his other writing than he is in *Transforming Mission,* which was designed for a global readership (14–21). For a recent view more favorable to Bosch's approach to contextualization, see Tiina Ahonen, *Transformation through Compassionate Mission: David J. Bosch's Theology of Contextualization* (Helsinki: Luther-Agricola-Society, 2003).

suppressed, and finally resurrected after Vatican II (131.9). It is remarkable that with all Bosch has to say about the importance of inculturation, the ideas and example of the Jesuit pioneers of inculturation (Xavier, de Nobili, and Ricci) are summarized in four lines on page 479. In fact, Asia as a whole hardly figures in Bosch's work at all, which is another huge gap.

Sugden, after noting the omission of Pentecostals and women, goes on to mention several other gaps — contextualized liturgical development (Catholic and Protestant), the environmental dimension of mission, and the role of Christian nongovernmental organizations (140.5; see also 149.7, which adds these to the list — Christian leadership, mission funding, the impact of the West on societies elsewhere, and the rejection of Western Christianity by the Islamic world). Some of these are practical and situational matters that naturally get overlooked when one takes an intellectual approach to the subject of mission (see criticism one above), but they are serious omissions. Readers should not assume that *Transforming Mission* has comprehensively covered the field of missiology.

3. Some outdated descriptions, such as the polarized contrast of ecumenicals and evangelicals

Verstraelen argues, "When dealing with contemporary models of mission Bosch remains completely captive to Western discussions on issues such as the relationship between ecumenical and evangelical Protestants" (20.4). This is a bit surprising since Bosch clearly shows that the whole polarization between ecumenicals and evangelicals is due to their differing reactions to the Enlightenment. The non-Western parts of the church have not been influenced by the Enlightenment to nearly the same extent, so they are not polarized nearly as badly. The more they contextualize the gospel (as Bosch says they should), the freer they will be from Enlightenment influences and the more the polarization problem will go away by itself. Why then does the problem loom so large in Bosch's thinking?

Cadorette points out a different weakness. In his view, Bosch's treatment of the idea of the preferential option for the poor and the development of base Christian communities is "condensed and decontextualized" (65.4) and his description of liberation theology in general is "succinct and somewhat dated" (67.3). Cadorette updates and fills in the picture.

B. NUSSBAUM'S PERSONAL REFLECTIONS ON BOSCH'S THEOLOGY OF MISSION AND ON DEVELOPMENTS IN MISSION, 1996–2004

My purpose on all pages of this book except the next few is to present Bosch's thought as objectively as possible. This does not mean I agree with it all, though I do come very close to that. It means I willingly accept the fact that the world is much more interested in Bosch's ideas than my reaction to them.

Nevertheless there are two reasons to add a few of my own thoughts at this point. First, no one can present a completely objective description of someone else's work. By sharing some of my own ideas here, I may enable the reader to watch out for my biases at other places in the book where they may have colored my description even though I did not realize or intend it. Second, Bosch did most of the writing of *Transforming Mission* in 1988–90, and the responses summarized above were mostly written in 1994–95. Readers today deserve at least a few observations on the current state of play in mission and missiology. I will focus on seven points that in my view were either absent or underrepresented in Bosch and the responses.

Before doing so, I wish to make one observation on Bosch's general procedure of reconciling apparently opposite positions and holding them together in "creative tension," a term that is sprinkled through his book at twenty-four different places. Some readers may have formed the mistaken impression that Bosch is so committed to the "creative tension" approach that he tries to include all possible positions in his new paradigm. While he is certainly a reconciler at heart, he does flatly reject some of the features of the old paradigms of mission. These are shown in bold italic in Table 14 (p. 147).

We thus see that Bosch is not a "peace at any price" person, nor one so open-minded that he considers all missiologies to be valid in their own way. He does have convictions and he argues for them, even though this means excluding many cherished missiological positions. He expects others to argue for their positions as well, and that is what I shall do now. He trained me to think, not to parrot.

1. The importance of the Pentecostals and the Orthodox for the emerging paradigm of mission

Since Bosch's main objective is to expose the Enlightenment to Christian criticism and help Western Christians think outside the Enlightenment box, the main surprise for me in the whole book is that Bosch pays so little attention to the two segments of global Christianity that have been least affected by the Enlightenment — the Orthodox and the Pentecostals.[4] He focuses instead on the Roman Catholics, the ecumenical Protestants, and the evangelical Protestants, the very groups that have been most affected by the Enlightenment.[5]

Is it not likely that some of the most penetrating and useful critiques of the influence of the Enlightenment and some of the most constructive alternatives would come from the churches in societies that have never been through the Enlightenment, never been secularized, never put their faith in technology, and

---

4. Saayman cited the omission of the Pentecostals as a major weakness in Bosch's work (see critique 2, p. 144), but I want to emphasize it here from a different angle.

5. He does outline the Orthodox paradigm of mission in one full chapter, but his critique of that paradigm is fairly sharp, and he does not draw on it much when he later presents his picture of the emerging paradigm.

Table 14
What Bosch Rejects

Bosch's sections[1]	Old paradigms	New paradigm
Church-with-others	***Mission is what we do to or for the world.***	Mission is what we do along with the world.
Missio Dei	***Church owns the mission***	God owns the mission
Mediating salvation	Various one-dimensional views	Comprehensive salvation
Quest for justice	Dichotomy of religion and justice	Convergence
Evangelism	Many separate narrow views	Complex, integrated
Contextualization (liberation and inculturation are sub-points)	***Theology from above aimed at educated unbeliever***	Theology from below aimed at poor unbeliever
Liberation	***Evolutionist; secularized***	Revolutionist; religious
Inculturation	***Western view is universally valid***	Local theologies
Common witness	***Either fragmentation or structural unity***	Diversity and unity
Whole people of God (laity)	***Control by clergy***	Affirmation of laity in mission
Witness to people of other faiths	Exclusivism, fulfillment or relativism	Creative tension
Theology	Missiology a compartment	Missionary theology
Action in hope	Eschatology everything or nothing	Eschatology and mission in tension

[1] The sections are listed here in order as they appear in *Transforming Mission*, not as I rearranged them in my description. See p. 92 for explanation of my regrouping.

never thought they could conquer the world? Christians there are bound to go about mission in a different way.

Of course, I am not saying that the Enlightenment has only affected white Christians and that the church in its mission will be free of the Enlightenment once the Christians of the ancient East or the global South are leading. For example, most of the current leaders of the church in the South were trained in Enlightenment-bound theological institutions in the North. Their training will not be undone in a day, nor should it be. However, if they can reconnect with their pre-Enlightenment roots (which at a few important points are similar to postmodernism), they can play a key role in ushering the church into the next stage of its mission.

2. The Walls shift: The global South in the driver's seat

The importance of Pentecostalism for a new paradigm of mission is reinforced by a shift in the global center of Christianity from the West to the South, as Scottish missiologist Andrew Walls has been emphasizing for decades now. Christian spiritual vitality, including the drive for mission and creative, mission-centered theology, is going along with that shift. Philip Jenkins's more recent book, *The Next Christendom,* has greatly raised awareness of these trends and their implications.

The demographic shift has continued, even accelerated, since Bosch's death in 1992. This is especially true in China, but not only there. The last decade has also seen the mushrooming of Protestant missionary-sending organizations in places like Korea, Brazil, India, Nigeria, and the Philippines and the enlistment of people from those countries into Roman Catholic missionary orders on a massive scale.

At the time of this writing we are beginning to see the church political implications of this demographic shift in the Anglican Communion. The part of the Anglican Church in the global South, now in the strong majority numerically, is asserting itself through global Anglican structures against the theological liberalism of Anglicans in the North. The same demographic shift may easily and soon have the same church political implications in every denominational family. This shift of political control in the churches will affect everything about missiology and mission from here on. The movers and the shakers will not be white, and the whites will not be movers and shakers. This is probably the biggest change in the church since the Reformation.

What might it mean for mission theology and practice? Let us consider just two examples with immense implications for every aspect of missiology.

A. The Philippines

In 2003 a national association of evangelical mission agencies in the Philippines began talking openly about a goal of sending two hundred thousand Filipino cross-cultural missionaries by the year 2010. By current models of mission, to recruit, train, fund, and supervise such a mission force is beyond the wildest dreams of feasibility, but the Filipinos are not sticking to current models. Instead, they will use self-funding, nonprofessional missionaries (mostly female domestic workers on contracts in south Asia or the Middle East) who will be backed as "missionaries" with prayer and encouragement by clusters of three or four congregations in the Philippines. These "missionaries" will gather in self-supervising teams for worship and mutual encouragement as they seek ways for appropriate witness in the homes or other places where they work. Since about a million Filipinos already work overseas and the Philippines as a nation is about 15 percent evangelical, a target of two hundred thousand is not as wild as it appears at first.

If mission (at least the part of it involving evangelism in largely non-Christian parts of the world) is to be done increasingly by a large number of nonprofessional "witnesses" rather than a small group of professional "missionaries," mission education and missiological writing will have to be overhauled. All these amateurs should be missiologically informed, but they are not going to read today's missiological journals. On the positive side, there will be many more organic connections between the grassroots Christians in the sending churches and the witnesses in the field. The idea of "missionary" will lose its unrealistic halo and become thinkable for many more Christians. And if the teams of witnesses are basically self-supervising on the field, anything can emerge from their witness — anything except a clergy-bound, institution-saddled, financially dependent local church.

B. The Ukraine

Two years after Bosch's death, a Nigerian Pentecostal missionary named Sunday Adelaja planted a church in the Ukraine, using the Russian language skills he had acquired while earning two degrees in communications at a university in Belarus. Nine years later, that congregation is the largest Pentecostal or evangelical congregation in Europe, with about 25,000 members, plus about 150 daughter congregations throughout the Ukraine and about 200 in other countries from the United States to the United Arab Emirates.[6]

Like the Filipinos, Adelaja was thinking outside the box, perhaps because he had not been schooled by Western Pentecostalism or Enlightenment influences to stay within the box. In fact, he is somewhat critical of Pentecostalism in Nigeria (largely a carbon copy of Western Pentecostalism) because it has so many millions of adherents and yet has not had much impact on the wider Nigerian society. He says that too many Pentecostals preach a "gospel of salvation" rather than the real, New Testament gospel, which is the "gospel of the kingdom."[7]

---

6. Sunday Adelaja, "Go to a Land That I Will Show You," in *Out of Africa: How the Spiritual Explosion among Nigerians Is Impacting the World*, ed. C. Peter Wagner and Joseph Thompson (Ventura, Calif.: Regal Books, 2003), 53.

7. These terms and the quotes in the next two paragraphs are based on personal notes from an address given by Adelaja at the "Light the Nation" conference at New Life Church, Colorado Springs,

He also does not use the street preaching and crusade methods that are common in Pentecostalism. Instead he teaches that according to the "gospel of the kingdom," each Christian has a God-given mission. Church members are to take the transforming influence (or "kingdom") of God into their assigned "land," that is, a segment of the community with which they are connected socially, through business, or in some other way. All members of Adelaja's church are required to participate in small groups, and all small groups revolve around "discovering your land" and being equipped and encouraged to take God's influence there.

The church runs a multitude of community service programs, such as drug rehabilitation and a weekly meal for over a thousand poor people. Says Adelaja, "What kind of a pastor am I if there are hungry people in my community and my church does nothing about it? What gospel am I preaching?"

All of this sounds very familiar to someone who has read Bosch (which I do not think Adelaja ever has). My point is that emerging Christian leaders from the global South may increasingly do what Bosch is calling for even though they never heard him call for it. It comes naturally to them, having had little influence from the Enlightenment. Their articulations of the gospel and their models of the church will shape the future of mission. What is more important for missiologists to study than that?

3. The kingdom announcement, demonstration, and teaching by Jesus

In his six-event Christological framework for the "many modes" of mission (chap. 13), Bosch (like most theologians) skips from the incarnation to the cross without mentioning Jesus' announcement of the kingdom, his teaching about the kingdom, or his miracles demonstrating the arrival of the kingdom. Given his emphases on the kingdom theme in chapter 1, it is surprising that he has confined it mostly to the "ascension" category in the framework in chapter 13 rather than treating it as a seventh category in its own right, between incarnation and crucifixion in his sequence.

Let us consider what is lost by this omission. Attention to Jesus' announcement of the arriving kingdom inescapably raises the question of healing miracles and other physical signs of a new spiritual power. Bosch notes these as significant aspects of Jesus' own mission (32.9–33.6, 107.1), but his emerging paradigm does not tell us how they fit into the mission of the church today, if at all. Nor does he say where or how healing miracles have disappeared from mission, if they have.

The biggest change I would make in Bosch's emerging paradigm would be to insert "healing" (including but not limited to physical healing) as a third main "activity of mission," parallel to evangelization and contextualization. I wonder

---

Colorado, October 23–25, 2003. The conference featured half a dozen senior Nigerian church leaders and missionaries.

whether the omission of healing from the model is not an example of the un-detected impact of Enlightenment thinking on Bosch himself. Healing is only a minor interest for the vast majority of scholars Bosch relies on, but they are operating for the most part within an Enlightenment framework. It is as hard to find a German New Testament scholar or theologian who has witnessed a con-vincing physical healing as it is to find a member of a Chinese house church or an African indigenous church who has not.

Miraculous physical healing does exactly what the Enlightenment says cannot be done — it demonstrates that the world of fact and the world of value cannot be kept separate and "religion" cannot be confined to the world of value. In other words, it reinforces Bosch's central thesis that the Enlightenment worldview is a seriously inadequate view of reality. In addition, Bosch's "creative tension" between the arriving power of the kingdom and the lingering weakness of the present would fit with the widely observed fact that some prayers for healing are answered and some are not. Healing deserves far more attention than Bosch gave it, and this can be done fairly simply without disrupting the rest of the model. Why not give healing its rightful place in the model?

4. The omission of the Gospel of John

I would love to know how Bosch decided he did not have room to include the mission theology of John. The influence of John on Christian mission has been massive and the perspective of John is so different from Matthew, Luke, and Paul that it seems impossible to me to weave the tapestry of a "New Testament" model of mission without using the Johannine threads as prominent parts of the picture.

John's form of the Great Commission (20:21) had an important influence in evangelical missiology in the 1970s and 1980s, pushing it away from an exclu-sively religious view of mission based on Matthew 28:19–20 and toward the more comprehensive view of salvation that Bosch advocates. Bosch was well aware of this but he does not tap John as a resource to build his case.[8] One of Bosch's favorite authors, Lesslie Newbigin, wrote a masterful commentary on the Gospel of John because he found John so useful in his presentation of the gospel to Hindus, but Bosch does not cite this work.[9]

What would the Gospel of John have added to Bosch's theology of mission? Its central question is whether Jesus is the Messiah or not. This has immense implications for our understanding of the relationship of Christianity to other faiths, which Bosch says is one of the two key unresolved issues for the church today (476.9). Is there a messiah figure in other faiths or not? If so, how does

---

8. Bosch has only a few passing references to John 20:20–23, and none of them is included in the chapter on his emerging paradigm. The only points he draws out from this text are the importance of suffering with Christ, receiving the Spirit, and forgiving sins (49.9, 66.1, 79.3, 513.9, 514.2)

9. Lesslie Newbigin, *The Light Has Come: An Exposition of the Fourth Gospel* (Grand Rapids: Eerdmans, 1982).

that messiah relate to Jesus the Messiah and to the Father who sent him? If not, how does an un-messianic faith relate to a messianic one?

Besides the messianic issue, John brings out the issue of Jesus' own sense of mission more clearly than any other gospel. Jesus is self-consciously a person on a mission, a person sent from God. John's theology uniquely presents Jesus the Messiah as the model of mission and the means by which others become missional people. John draws an analogy between the relationship of Jesus to the Father and the relationship of Jesus' followers to him. This is brought out in at least six places, climaxing in John's version of the Great Commission:

- "Just as the living Father sent me and I live because of the Father, so the one who feeds on me will live because of me" (6:57).

- "...I know my sheep and my sheep know me — just as the Father knows me and I know the Father" (10:14–15).

- "As the Father has loved me, so have I loved you" (15:9, cf. 13:15 and 34).

- "If you obey my commands, you will remain in my love, just as I have obeyed my Father's commands and remain in his love" (15:10.)

- "...just as you [the Father] are in me and I am in you. May they also be in us so that the world may believe that you have sent me" (17:21, cf. 14:20).

- "As the Father has sent me, I am sending you" (20:21, cf. 17:18).

As Bosch presented Matthew's version of the Great Commission as the integrating finale of his entire gospel, one can imagine him doing an equally insightful thing with John 20:21. What an exposition that would have made! But we will have to rely on others for help with John's theology and missiology.

5. Postmodernism (anti-ideology) vs. the last ideology still standing (capitalism)?

When Bosch wrote *Transforming Mission,* the Soviet Union was still in one piece, Nelson Mandela was still in jail, and postmodernism was still a vague new concept for most people. Though the ideologies of communism and apartheid (South African Nazism) were still not finished off, it was pretty clear that capitalism would be the one great ideology left standing by the end of the twentieth century. But the relation of capitalism to postmodernism was not clear, and still is not.

Capitalism is driving the phenomenon of globalization, which has been so much studied in recent years. The backlash to globalization is localization (or global Balkanization), described by Benjamin Barber in *Jihad vs. McWorld.* But another enemy lurks much closer to the home of capitalism, and that enemy is postmodernism.

Capitalism is modern. Like the other "Great Ideologies" Bosch describes — communism, Nazism, and Fascism (see 359.4) — capitalism is a child of the

Enlightenment and it has the confidence that it can calculate life, conquer the world, and make it a better place. It also is totalitarian (demanding that every aspect of life revolve around it). Unlike the other "Great Ideologies" it exercises its control through economic rather than political structures.

Postmodernism is anti-modern and theoretically ought to be anti-capitalist. Postmoderns do not believe in any "grand metanarrative," such as the capitalist myth that market forces will solve the world's problems if governments would just trust capitalism itself and quit passing laws and regulations that get in the way. To postmoderns, that myth is just a fig leaf to cover the moral nakedness of the power holders. Postmoderns would rather have capitalists admit the (supposed) truth they do not care about the welfare of the world. They are only in it for the money.

And yet postmoderns invest in the stock market, claiming that for them the market is only an economic mechanism and not part of any grand scheme of things. It makes money (or loses it) but it is not the god it claims to be. By this intellectual maneuver, postmoderns sterilize capitalistic theory and yet leave the door open for themselves to benefit personally from the capitalist structures of their choice. They are not capitalists but capitalizers.

6. Goodbye Christendom, hello sharia-dom?

There is no safer whipping-boy among missiologists today than the concept of Christendom. No one is for it. The long derided Anabaptist view of the separation of church and state has finally become the majority view, and certainly the view Bosch advocates.[10] True mission does not impose itself through political power.

How ironic that just as Christians agree to bury the concept of Christendom, radical Muslims emerge on a mission to expand "sharia-dom." The desire of many of these radicals is to impose Islam by law if possible and by violence if necessary, first on predominantly Muslim societies and eventually on the whole world.

Bosch has a lot to say about the "Great Ideologies" rooted in the Enlightenment but little or nothing on ideologies rooted in pre-Enlightenment religions such as Islam and Hinduism. There is the intriguing possibility that had he lived to see the emergence of these religious ideologies as major factors in national and global politics, he may have critiqued them in either of two ways. He may have seen them as perversions of the religions they supposedly represent, drawing an analogy with South African apartheid as a perversion of Christianity (a heresy). On the other hand, he may have seen them as logical outcomes of those religious systems and critiqued the core doctrines of Islam and Hinduism because they

---

10. Though Bosch criticizes the "Christendom" approach to mission, Saayman says he is disappointed that Bosch was not more critical of the "Constantinian reversal" in his section on the Orthodox paradigm of mission. Saayman believes the shift had huge implications centuries later for the theology of colonialism, which seriously compromised the mission of the Western churches (*Bold Humility*, 45.3).

could produce such ideologies. Or, more likely, he might have found a way to hold those two views in creative tension!

7. Pluralism: Tolerance as the new dividing line among Christians?

Bosch believed that the relation of Christianity to other faiths is one of the two key issues for missiology today (476.9). He advocates "creative tension" in our understanding, but the tension is growing year by year and the creativity does not seem to be keeping up with it. It would not surprise me if a new division emerged within Christianity, cutting across all denominational families.

The dividing line, ironically, may be the issue of tolerance when it comes to mission practice toward members of other faiths. The question could be framed this way: "What does genuine 'mission' have to do with Christians attempting to persuade non-Christians that they should become Christians?" The exclusivists will say that is the essential core of mission. The relativists will say that mission has nothing to do with that mistaken idea. The fulfillment group will have a more complex answer, perhaps that Christians should witness with this in view but not draw any theological conclusions about non-Christians who are not persuaded.

Of course, the whole discussion begs the question of what is a "Christian" or a "non-Christian." But when the discussion reaches that point and mutually exclusive definitions are put forward, division is probably not far away. However, there is another distinct possibility besides division. It is that the more evangelistic Christians in the Two-Thirds World will simply ignore the pluralists in the West, not considering it worthwhile to debate them, condemn them, or divide from them. Bosch would not have wanted to see such a breakdown, and he has tried mightily to identify enough common ground that the two views can be reconciled. It remains to be seen if that ground will hold or be eroded by the floods of the new era that the church and the world are entering.

YOUR VIEWS AND YOUR CONTEXT

92. Suppose your teacher assigns each student to choose and read two articles in *Mission in Bold Humility*. Which two will you read and why?

93. Which of the four "major contributions" of Bosch listed in Part A above do you value the most? Describe its impact on your thinking.

94. Which of the three criticisms of Bosch do you think is most serious? What weaknesses, if any, does this criticism reveal in Bosch's emerging paradigm?

95. Comment on any one of my seven reflections on Bosch, whichever you think is of most importance to the future of mission.

96. List three points, topics, or quotes from any section of *Transforming Mission* that have been most helpful and memorable to you. Briefly state how they have stimulated or changed your own thinking.

97. List two topics covered or mentioned in *Transforming Mission* that you want to study more. What is the practical importance of these two for your future in God's mission?

98. Write a one-paragraph prayer that amplifies the classic biblical prayer about mission, "Your kingdom come" (Matt. 6:10).

Appendix A: Table 15

Twentieth-Century Mission Conferences and Documents

	1900	1920	1940	1960	1980
Ecumenical	***Edinburgh 1910***				
International Missionary Council		Jerusalem 1928 Tambaram 1938	Willingen 1952		
World Council of Churches			Whitby 1947 Achimota 1958	***Delhi 1961*** Uppsala 1968 Nairobi 1975	Vancouver 1983
WCC mission & evangelism dept.				Bangkok 1973	Melbourne 1980 San Antonio 1989
Evangelical				Berlin 1966 ***Lausanne 1974***	Pattaya 1980 Manila 1989
Roman Catholic	Maximum Illud 1919	Rerum Ecclesiae 1926	Fidei Donum 1957	***Vatican II 1962-65 (Lumen Gentium; Ad Gentes)*** Evangelii Nuntiandi 1975	

Note: the four crucial meetings of the century are shown in bold italic. Meetings after 1990, when Bosch wrote, are not shown.

Appendix B

Authors Most Quoted by David Bosch

Missiologists (general)

Anderson, Gerald H. (1930–), American, Methodist, mission experience in the Philippines, director of the Overseas Ministries Study Center and editor of the *International Bulletin of Missionary Research* for twenty-five years (1976–2000). With his wide-ranging interest in history and theology of mission and his wide contacts across the whole spectrum of denominations, he has edited or co-edited a number of major mission volumes, such as the *Concise Dictionary of Christian World Missions*. He is the only person in this list of "Authors Most Quoted by Bosch" who has also contributed an essay to the volume of responses to Bosch, *Mission in Bold Humility* (see chapter 14 above).

Hiebert, Paul (1932–), American anthropologist and missiologist, Mennonite, mission experience in India. He has taught both at Fuller Theological Seminary (Los Angeles) and since 1990 at Trinity International University (Chicago). He is one of the main advocates in the evangelical camp for "critical contextualization." Bosch is interested both in his views on contextualization and his writing on the relationship between postmodern epistemology and missiology.

Neill, Stephen (1900–1984), Scottish, Anglican, child of missionary parents, mission experience in India as a Bible translator, evangelist, ecumenist, and bishop. Neill was an expert in Tamil culture and engaged in extensive dialogue with Hindus. In later life he wrote profusely on the history, theology, and practice of mission. Bosch refers to him frequently both in his historical section and in the section on the emerging paradigm.

Rosenkranz, Gerhard (1896–1966), German, staff member then director of German East Asia Mission 1931–48, including a year of field study and interreligious dialogue in China, Korea, and Japan. Influenced by Otto (phenomenology of religion) and Althaus (realized eschatology). He is one of the few who attempt to cover both the history and theology of mission as Bosch does. Thus Bosch refers to him on a wide range of topics.

Scherer, James A. (1926–), American Lutheran, mission experience in China and Japan, professor of mission and church history at Lutheran School of Theology, Chicago, 1957–92. Wide-ranging references to him, as to Neill and Rosenkranz above.

Sundermeier, Theo (1935–), German, mission experience in Namibia and South Africa, professor of mission and history of religions at Heidelberg. Specialist in theology of religion, but has contributed on a number of other missiological topics as well.

Mission historians

Chaney, Charles L. (1934–), American, Southern Baptist, specialist in church planting in North America. His book on American mission history is a major source for Bosch's description of the American version of "Mission in the Wake of the Enlightenment" (chap. 9).

Hutchison, William R. (1930–), American, professor of North American religious history at Harvard Divinity School. Chaney gives the conservative perspective on American mission history; Hutchison (a member of the Unitarian Universalist Historical Society) gives the more liberal one. Bosch uses both in his chapter on the history of modern mission (chap. 9) but refers to Hutchison more often when he presents his own paradigm (chap. 13), since Hutchison has more to say about ideology and mission.

Van den Berg, Johannes (1922–), Dutch, specialist in early mission history in Britain. Bosch quotes him mostly in the chapter on mission after the Enlightenment.

Walls, Andrew F. (1928–), Scottish, Methodist, mission experience in Sierra Leone and Nigeria, probably the most highly respected of living mission historians. He founded and directed the Centre for the Study of Christianity in the Non-Western World, now at the University of Edinburgh. His overarching theme for decades has been the significance of the shift of the Christian heartland from the West to the South, particularly Africa, during the twentieth century.

Mission theologians

Gensichen, Hans-Werner (1915–99), German, Lutheran, mission experience in India as a teacher. From 1957 he was professor of the history of religions and missiology at the University of Heidelberg. Bosch lists ten different works of his (mostly German) in the bibliography. He quotes him frequently and agrees with him nearly all the time.

Hoekendijk, J. C. (1912–75), Dutch, born in Indonesia to missionary parents. After brief mission service in Indonesia himself, he returned to the Netherlands because of ill health. He emerged as a leading spokesperson for those who believed mission should be secularized, with emphasis shifted from the church to the world. Bosch believed he had gone too far in that direction. He quotes him more than anyone else he disagrees with.

Kraemer, Hendrik (1888–1965), Dutch lay missionary, linguist, and scholar. His book *The Christian Message in a Non-Christian World* was one of the most influential of the century. He was the first director of the Ecumenical Institute at Bossey, Switzerland. Bosch regarded him as a significant thinker in a previous era whose ideas still have some relevance today.

Newbigin, Lesslie (1909–98), British missiologist, mission experience in India, conservative ecumenical (United Reformed). In the 1980s and 1990s he took a leading role in the "Gospel and Culture" movement in Britain, promoting a missionary encounter of the gospel with Western culture in general and the negative effects of the Enlightenment on the church in particular. Bosch considered his book *The Open Secret: Sketches for a Missionary Theology* perhaps the best introduction to the subject. Many of his works are available at www.newbigin.net.

Rütti, Ludwig (1936–), German, Catholic on the staff of the Institute for Mission Studies in Munich. None of his work has appeared in English translation, but Bosch considers him a very important mission thinker. Occasionally his views are too radical to suit Bosch's own framework.

New Testament scholars

Beker, J. Christiaan (1924–99), Dutch-born American, professor at Princeton Theological Seminary 1964–94, a Pauline specialist acknowledged as one of the most significant American New Testament scholars in the last half of the twentieth century. Bosch relies more on his interpretation of Paul than any other scholar's.

Hahn, Ferdinand (1926–), German, professor of New Testament at Munich 1976–94, with interest in how the many strands of New Testament theology compare and contrast with one another, especially when it comes to mission. Bosch's chapters on Matthew and Paul as well as his overview of the New Testament make extensive use of Hahn's work.

Hengel, Martin (1926–), German, conservative, specialist in the influence of Hellenism on Judaism. Professor at Tübingen.

Käsemann, Ernst (1906–98), German, studied under Bultmann. He was both radical and influential in the field of New Testament studies, particularly in his work on the historical Jesus and his interpretation of Romans.

Malherbe, Abraham J. (1930–), American, evangelical (Church of Christ member and pastor), professor of New Testament at Yale 1964–94. Bosch appreciates his work on Paul and on the social setting of early Christianity.

Sanders, E. P. (1937–), American expert in first-century Judaism, especially in relation to Jesus and Paul. He has taught at McMaster, Oxford, and Duke.

Schottroff, Luise (1934–), German, considered to be Europe's leading feminist New Testament scholar, with more than twenty books to her credit. She is now retired from New Testament professorship at the University of Kassel. Bosch frequently quotes the book she co-wrote with W. Stegemann. She is the only woman in this list of thirty-two authors.

Senior, Donald (1940–), American, professor at Catholic Theological Union, Chicago. Bosch considered the book he wrote with his colleague Carroll Stuhl-mueller to be the book that came closest to laying the foundations for a biblical theology of mission, yet he did not think the book did enough building on those foundations. Bosch considered writing something himself that would go further, but it was not to be.

Pre-twentieth century

Augustine of Hippo (354–430), North African, possibly the single most influential theologian in the history of the Western church. A pastor and bishop in what is now Tunisia, he helped the Western church reshape its theology and worldview to account for the fall of Rome (410). Bosch regards him as the defining figure for the medieval Roman Catholic paradigm of mission even though he predated the Middle Ages by two centuries.

Luther, Martin (1483–1546), German, initiator and a main leader of the Protestant Reformation. As a German Catholic priest, he was so insistent on the doctrine of justification by faith and so critical of the church that he was excommunicated in 1520. With the backing of much of the German nobility, he then established the church that came to bear his name. He translated the Bible into German, wrote hymns, and continued his preaching and university work to the end of his life. Though Bosch is in the Calvinist tradition, Luther occurs fifteen times in his index and Calvin only ten.

Warneck, Gustav (1834–1910), German scholar considered "the father of German missiology," writer of the first comprehensive German theology of mission. Poor health prevented him from becoming a missionary himself, but he served as an administrator for the Rhenish Mission and was a key figure in establishing mission periodicals, mission conferences, and associations.

Theologians (general)

Barth, Karl (1886–1968), Swiss, probably the most influential Protestant theologian of the twentieth century. He was the father of neo-orthodoxy and the opponent of classic liberalism. Bosch frequently takes one of Barth's ideas as a starting point and develops his own ideas around it.

Gutiérrez, Gustavo (1928–), Peruvian, Roman Catholic, the leading pioneer of the Latin American liberation theology movement. He is the only non-Western writer included in this list of those Bosch quotes most.

Küng, Hans (1928–), Swiss, Roman Catholic, a prolific writer with immense influence from his professor's position at the University of Tübingen since 1963. Though he has raised some serious questions about his church, he has remained (and been permitted to remain) a loyal Catholic. Bosch adopts his outline of six phases in church history and develops his six paradigms of mission around them.

Moltmann, Jürgen (1926–), German, best known for his emphasis on hope as a key concept in Christian theology. Like Hans Küng, he joined the theology faculty at Tübingen in 1963. He is referred to very frequently in the chapter where Bosch sketches the emerging paradigm of mission.

Niebuhr, H. Richard (1894–1962), American, influenced by Barth and Troeltsch. His most influential book was *Christ and Culture,* sketching five models of the relationship between Christ and culture. Bosch, however, does not quote that book. He draws on Niebuhr for his histories of the Social Gospel and the Kingdom of God in America.

Stackhouse, Max (1935–), American, ethicist, United Church of Christ (ecumenical), teaching experience in India and Fiji. Professor at Princeton Theological Seminary, specializing in the relationship of theological ethics to society. Like Moltmann, he is very frequently referred to in Bosch's chapter on the emerging paradigm.

Index

Numbers in *italics* indicate figures

**Previously published in
the American Society of Missiology Series**

24. *Dictionary of Mission: Theology, History, Perspectives*, edited by Karl Müller, Theo Sundermeier, Stephen B. Bevans, and Richard H. Bliese

25. *Earthen Vessels and Transcendent Power: American Presbyterians in China, 1837–1952*, G. Thompson Brown

26. *The Missionary Movement in American Catholic History, 1820–1980*, Angelyn Dries

27. *Missions in the New Testament: An Evangelical Approach*, edited by William J. Larkin Jr. and Joel W. Williams

28. *Changing Frontiers of Missions*, Wilbert Shenk

29. *In the Light of the Word: Divine Word Missionaries of North America*, Ernest Brandewie

30. *Constants in Context: Theology of Mission for Today*, Stephen B. Bevans and Roger Schroeder

31. *Changing Tides: Latin America and Mission Today*, Samuel Escobar

32. *Gospel Bearers, Gender Barriers: Missionary Women in the Twentieth Century*, edited by Dana L. Robert

33. *Church: Community for the Kingdom*, John Fuellenbach

34. *Mission in Acts: Ancient Narratives for a Postmodern Context*, edited by Robert L. Gallager and Paul Hertig

35. *A History of Christianity in Asia: Vol. 1, Beginnings to 1500*, Samuel Hugh Moffett

36. *A History of Christianity in Asia: Vol. 2, 1500–1900*, Samuel Hugh Moffett